THE CIVIL ADV...  ...OK

by

Ronald E Conway
Solicitor Advocate
Bonnar Accident Law
ronniec@bonnarandco.com; www.bonnaraccidentlaw.com

and

Bridget McCann
Presentation and Communication Skills Trainer
bridget.mccann1@googlemail.com; www.bridgetmccanntrainer.com

with

Claire Anne MacFadden
Solicitor
J K Cameron Solicitors, Glasgow

The Civil Advocacy Skills Book

Published in 2015 in Scotland by Concann Productions Limited, a paperback original.

© Ronald E Conway and Bridget McCann

Ronald E Conway and Bridget McCann have asserted their individual moral rights to be identified as authors of this work.

Cover designed by Brian McGuffie, g3Creative, Glasgow
Typeset by Frances Hendron, Hendron Associates, Glasgow
Printed and bound by Charlesworth Press, Wakefield

All QR exercises can also be accessed at www.bridgetmccanntrainer.com

ISBN 978 0 9931848 0 2

CONTENTS

		page
	Acknowledgements	4
	How to get the best out of this book	5

Part One
	Introduction, Ronald E Conway	6
1.	Proof Preparation	9
2.	Appearing in Court, the Rules and Rituals	19
3.	The Basic Dynamics of Advocacy	27
4.	Examination-in-Chief	32
5.	The Organisation of the Examination-in-Chief	42
6.	Cross-Examination	51
7.	Objections	63
8.	Expert Witnesses	69
9.	The Hearing on Evidence	79
10.	Incidental and Procedure Roll Advocacy	83
11.	Appellate Advocacy	89
12.	Family and Domestic Relations Advocacy	97
13.	Final Words – A Practice Regime	111

Part Two
	Introduction, Bridget McCann	146
14.	Anxiety	148
15.	Relaxation	156
16.	Breathing	161
17.	Posture	171
18.	Voice	182
19.	Body Language	203
20.	Preparation	212

Appendices
	Exercises		218
	Shared Experience:	(1) Actors	234
		(2) Lawyers	238
	Bibliographies		253

ACKNOWLEDGEMENTS

We would warmly like to thank the following:

Frances Hendron – Editor extraordinaire for working wonders weaving two stories into one
Claire Anne McFadden for shining a light on the complexities of Family Law Advocacy
Mary McFarlane the quintessential without whom…..
Andy Ward, proof reader for Ronnie
Great Scot Photography for Cover Photography
g3creative.co.uk for Cover Design
Recording2U for QR Video Recording, Editing and Post Production www.recording2u.co.uk
Rich Chapman Thoughtcrime Media Sound for QR Sound Inserts firewallsound@gmail.com
Rachel Conway and Kieran Baker – QR Actors
Martha Leishman – QR Voiceover Artiste
Susan Clark, Legal Services Agency
Rob Casement
Anne Conway
Kirsty Wark
Carol Ann Crawford

HOW TO GET THE BEST OUT OF THIS BOOK

This book is unique in that it offers you not only a comprehensive insight into understanding the facets of Civil Advocacy, but also how best to present yourself in a professional manner.

You should first read Part 1, which we consider to be the *what* of Civil Advocacy before you read Part 2, which is the *how to*. In Part 2 we also use QR reader exercises to show as well as tell how you can transform yourselves into relaxed and articulate court practitioners.

At the end of Part 1 we have included a chapter on an area of the law which many of you may find relevant. Claire Anne McFadden offers her extensive personal experience of Family and Domestic Relations Advocacy.

We have also called upon the expertise of eminent QCs and solicitor advocates who have generously offered up some pearls of wisdom distilled from many years in court.

Unfortunately there are no shortcuts. But please trust us that everything succumbs to practice. To make the most of this book, you should read and think about the text, access the speech and advocacy exercises, and then practise them again and again.

Ronald E Conway
and Bridget McCann

Abbreviations
SCR – Summary Cause Rules
OCR – Ordinary Cause Rules
QR – Quick Response code generator (for bar codes linked to exercises on YouTube)

PART ONE by Ronald E Conway

INTRODUCTION

"I am calling you as a matter of courtesy to say that this proof will be proceeding."

You put the phone down.

The doors on the last-chance settlement saloon have just swung shut. To paraphrase P.G. Wodehouse, a swarm of butterflies has suddenly decamped from a nearby meadow, and set up residence in the pit of your stomach. Bridget has ideas which will help you deal with these worries, but you are right to be nervous. There is generally no middle way in litigation. It is win or lose. If there is a client who believes in the Kipling line that triumph and disaster are much the same, I have yet to meet him. Your own capabilities as a trial lawyer are about to be tested in an arena which can be brutal and unforgiving. A civil proof is not an inquiry after truth but a presentation, both of the facts of the case and of yourself. We have all seen lawyers at work for whom advocacy seems to come very easily. They dominate witnesses by force of personality, their quicksilver minds effortlessly expose contradiction and inconsistencies in testimony, they have the ear of the court.

Very few of us are blessed with these high gifts of nature (and it is a mistake to assume that they come to anyone without labour) and our aspirations should be rather more modest; to acquire a level of competence which enables us to present the cases entrusted to us as effectively as possible. This is a skill. It depends partly on natural ability, but much more significantly on technique and practice. It is a skill which can be learned by anyone with the inclination and determination consistently to spend time on it. And like a tennis forehand, you cannot acquire this skill simply by reading about it or playing things over in your head.

Introduction

A further paradox is that whilst experience is necessary, it is not enough. Emergency rescue pilots talk of their 300 hours flying time, and dismiss those of their number who have repeated the same 1 hour 300 times. There are simple rules and guidelines for the examination of witnesses and presentation of evidence which can educate and inform your experience.

What is different about this book on advocacy is the emphasis on personal projection and presence which Bridget McCann can bring. As a successful actor, trainer and consultant, she has for a number of years cast a practiced eye over the efforts of lawyers to make the most of themselves in court. Most legal training concentrates on the 'what' of the law. Bridget covers the 'how'. Her passion is to help the young and inexperienced to become effective courtroom communicators by passing on tips and techniques learnt working in theatre.

Through her years of running advocacy skills workshops at The Legal Services Agency, Strathclyde Law School and leading law firms, she has seen the difficulties preventing young lawyers from doing themselves justice in court. In this modern world many young people communicate principally by text message, and have little or no practice at public speaking. The demise of reading aloud, debating societies, and of any opportunity for formal presentations, has produced a generation who present themselves in an inappropriate manner, with poor posture and fast, mumbled speech whenever they are placed in a formal setting.

In this book Bridget aims to offer clear and practical advice as to how to achieve the skills necessary to present a compelling case in the courtroom.

She will address the serious problem of 'stage fright'; explaining it and looking at ways to harness and manage it. (*The Flower and the Candle* exercise is worth the cover price of this book on its own.)

Bridget will look at the close link between, the body, mind and voice in terms of 'performance'. She will show that the mental approach to appearing in court is as important as preparing the brief. She will also introduce the idea of a physical warm-up, showing that it is as important to a lawyer's appearance in court, as it would be to a runner before a race.

Introduction

Much of Bridget's contribution to this book will be looking at the voice. She promotes the importance of breathing correctly, so that the voice is supported. She will offer exercises to improve diction. She will lay out all the vocal skills used by actors to enable the audience to follow the story and remain engaged.

Her emphasis on warm up, diction and voice projection, through breathing is unique in legal advocacy literature.

The Courts Reform (Scotland) Act 2014 places the sheriff court firmly at the centre of the litigation process, and this book is written for the lawyers who will work there.

If you follow (and practise) the ideas in this book, you will elevate yourselves to the ranks of the competent.

Whether you go on to achieve mastery, is a matter for you.

(Readers should note that all gender references have been randomly generated.)

1 Proof Preparation

"Effective lawyering boils down to hard work and preparation. One of the beauties of the law and one of its curses is that there is no limit to how much you can do to prepare a case. You can always dig for more information, you can always spend more time mastering the facts and the evidence, you can always learn more about the law. In the end success is a direct function of how much desire and commitment you have"

Daniel Petrocelli *Triumph of Justice:*
The Final Judgement on the Simpson Saga,
Random House, 1998.

Petrocelli was the lawyer who successfully won $8.5 million US damages for the family of Ron Goldman in the civil case against O. J. Simpson, after the criminal prosecution failed.

You will read a lot in this book about the importance of organisation, be it of documents, exhibits or self. Put simply, a proof is taxing enough without increasing that stress by frantically assembling papers and productions on the morning, and having to commence your preliminary remarks to the court with a catalogue of excuses for procedural failures.

Case Analysis – The Pleadings

The pleadings are your first port of call in any proof preparation. They contain the material facts on which the parties rely, but not the evidence to prove those facts. Specification may now be required in only general terms, and in personal injury actions may be provided by information contained in e.g. the statement of valuation. Parties are entitled to prosecute their case on the basis that the issues have been defined by the pleadings, and are limited to those identified there. So where there is no allegation of contributory negligence in the answers, no evidence can be led on the subject at proof.

Proof Preparation

This is not the place for a detailed discussion of the elements of pleading style but a few general remarks are appropriate. The record will be the first thing the sheriff reads before a word of evidence is led. It is your first opportunity to argue the case. Don't waste it by presenting a sloppy, disorganised and difficult to follow set of written pleadings. Don't plead the case too high. The written pleadings represent the promise on the facts which both parties make, and you can be sure that you will be held to yours at the conclusion of the evidence. If anything, undersell at this stage. Drop all adverbs and needless adjectives and present an understated recitation of the facts you are confident will emerge, without resort to exaggeration or rhetoric.

Case Analysis – The Facts

It is the duty of the modern judge to give reasons for his decision. It is the duty of the modern advocate to provide the judge with those reasons. The content of this duty will vary depending on the nature of the findings in fact. So where, for example, the issue is, "Did A punch B?", not much more may be required than a finding that B in demeanour was credible and reliable, and A was not. At the other end of the spectrum where expert evidence is involved the judge should engage with it and provide a reasoned basis for its acceptance or rejection.[1] Civil cases are decided on the balance of probabilities i.e. the 51% test, but this test does not apply to every critical fact in the course of the proof. Instead at the end of the case, the judge will look at the whole evidence on a probabilistic basis.[2] So the way that facts fit in with other facts is critical. In most cases the court will be faced with two alternative stories and will be asked to prefer one over the other.[3] There is a category of case where the quality of evidence is so poor or all versions so inherently improbable that the court may deal with matters on a burden of proof basis. But the authorities make it plain that such cases are extremely rare, so don't let your opponent frame the issue as a burden of proof point.[4]

---

[1] *Flannery v. Halifax Estate Agencies Limited* [2000] 1 W.L.R. 377
[2] *Karanakaran v. Secretary of State for the Home Department* [2000] 3 All E.R. 449
[3] *Ide v. ATB Sales Ltd* [2008] EWCA Civ 424.
[4] *Jenkins v. Allied Iron Founders Ltd.*, 1970 S.C. (H.L.) 37.

Core Factual Matrix

In every case there will be a core of undisputed or undeniable facts. The battleground will be the penumbra of the facts and circumstances around that core. The court will apply the normal rules of probability and plausibility to the facts and to causation. The art of persuasion for you as advocate is to marshal and assemble the evidence in a manner which inexorably forces the judge to find the probabilities in your favour.

What makes a good story? In a withering critique of James Fenimore Cooper's "The Deer Slayer",[5] Mark Twain set out some dramatic canons which hold true today. Twain found that *The Deer Slayer* was seriously lacking in in all of the following:

- The story shall accomplish something and go somewhere.
- The episodes in the story should be necessary parts of it and should help develop it.
- The persons in the story should exhibit a sufficient reason for their presence.
- The persons in the story should act in character.
- The persons in the story should confine themselves to probabilities or possibilities and should let miracles alone.
- The persons in the story should elicit a natural sympathy and the desire that justice should be done to them and for them.

Think of successful TV soaps such as Eastenders or Coronation Street which millions watch each week because of storylines based on character driven actions. Your client's story should have similar dynamics, if a bit less sensational.

Many of the controversial facts are bound to be more probable than not, once they are put in the context of the Core Factual Matrix. It is your task to bring the evidence to bear which will populate that Matrix with the facts favourable to your side. All the other evidence will then be assessed in that context.

---

[5] *Fenimore Cooper's Literary Offenses*", Mark Twain 1895.

Proof Preparation

The Trial Notebook

This should be a mid-sized lever arch folder, with the contents divided by separators. The Trial Notebook is separate from the full litigation folders, which contain all pleadings, productions and interlocutors. A Trial Notebook enables you to deal with and respond immediately to any evidential points as they arise. The sections are as follows:-

1. *An up to date record*
   You should also have ready a proposed record if there is a late minute of amendment to be proffered.

2. *A list of all the pursuer's and defenders' productions*
   This should also have the process number and a description of the document set out in an easily comprehensible fashion, double spaced and printed on font size 16. The objective is to enable the advocate to know and identify immediately the critical documents by process number. The productions themselves should be in a separate litigation folder.

3. *A set of the actual documents which you will be using in cross-examination*
   In almost every case there will be documents which you will want to put to certain witnesses in cross. Put post-it notes at the particular pages to which you intend to refer. These might be signed witness statements, accident reports completed by the witness, or particular pages in medical records. Effective cross-examination depends on these documents being at your fingertips so have copies in the cross-examination section of the Trial Notebook, as well as the normal litigation folders. These might already be lodged in inventories but it is not necessary to do so if their only purpose is cross-examination, and you will lose any element of surprise if they are in process.[6]

4. *Your outline submissions*
   For the advocate a proof is a presentation, not a truth finding inquiry at large, although you should always proceed with the sheriff on the basis that

---

[6] *Robertson v. Anderson* [CSOH] 15th May 2001.

his role is not simply fact finding but truth and justice finding. You should prepare an outline submission which contains the crucial findings in fact which you are confident will emerge, and the legal arguments which support your case. This will not be your actual submission, because every case will have unexpected twists and turns which you cannot anticipate, but it is your map, and you should navigate by dead reckoning.

5. *A chronology*
Each case will have critical facts being spoken to by different witnesses at different times. There is no more salutary discipline than setting these out in a simple timeline showing the facts and the evidential source of the facts. What you are trying to do is to change the temporal structure into a story. So evidence that A happened, then B happened, then C happened is simply a timeline e.g. "The Queen's daughter contracted the plague and died. The Queen then died. Then the King died six months later."

This is not a story. But consider:

> "The Queen's daughter caught the plague and died. The Queen was at her bedside, contracted the plague and only survived her by a few weeks. The King died of a broken heart six months later."[7]

That is a story with a plot and causes and effects. There is no better way of highlighting motivation, actions and causality than by closely focussing on the temporalities in the story. If the case is complicated, think about investing in a software programme such as CaseMap which enables detailed timelines to be plotted.

6. *The advocacy witness statements*
A set of precognitions does not provide easily accessible information in the format which you will require whilst examining witnesses. The advocacy witness statements are the detailed essence of the precognitions, drafted by you for each important witness in direct and cross-examination. These should be in font size 16 and double spaced. We will return to the format when we look at examination and cross-examination.

---

[7] This example is adapted from *"Aspects of the Novel"* by E.M. Forster, 1927.

Proof Preparation

7. *Legal authorities*
    These will be both the cases to which you will be referring the court during submissions, and also the evidential authorities which may be required during the course of the proof. Think about the areas where objection to your evidence might arise, or where you intend to object to evidence likely to be led by your opponent. If there are relevant authorities, highlight the pages and have them ready in triplicate. You will be proffering the cases both to the court and to your opponent.

Sources of evidence

In general terms the materials you will have are as follows:

- Oral evidence including expert evidence.
- Documentary evidence.
- Demonstrative evidence such as photographs.
- Real evidence where corporeal things are actually brought to the court.

There is a hierarchy of importance here. The strength of oral evidence will vary greatly according to the status and independence of the witness, his opportunity for observation and his powers of recollection. Young lawyers are surprised to learn that oral evidence is frequently not the most important source in civil cases. You should first of all look to any documentary evidence, particularly where the papers have been drawn up contemporaneously. You must exhaust the discovery process to obtain all relevant documents. Think about what might have been recorded and where and draft a specification of documents for its recovery. An initial accident report made at the time is far more likely to contain the unvarnished truth than oral witness evidence years after the event. What a claimant said about his accident circumstances at his first hospital attendance, when focussed on his health and treatment, is much more important than his now different story at proof.

In a case where there was widely differing oral evidence, the Privy Council put the matter this way:

"In such a case, memories may very well be unreliable: and it is of crucial importance for the Judge to have regard to the contemporary documents and to the overall probabilities. In this connection their Lordships wish to endorse a passage from one of their number in *Armagas Ltd. v. Mundogas S. A. (The Ocean Frost)*, [1985] 1 Lloyds Rep. 1 when he said at page 57:

> 'Speaking from my own experience I have found it essential in cases of fraud when considering the credibility of witnesses, always to test their veracity by reference to the objective facts proved independently of their testimony, in particular by reference to the documents in the case, and also to pay particular regard to their motives and to the overall probabilities. It is frequently very difficult to tell whether a witness is telling the truth or not: and where there is a conflict of evidence such as there was in the present case, reference to the objective facts and documents, to the witnesses' motives, and to the overall probabilities can be of very great assistance to a Judge in ascertaining the truth.'

That observation is, in their Lordships' opinion, equally apposite in a case where the evidence of the witnesses is likely to be unreliable."[8]

Photographs

Wherever possible make liberal use of photographs. Nothing else has quite their impact. There is a significantly greater retention of visual as opposed to verbal information.

Physical objects

Finally consider bringing the physical item to the court. If you are saying that the shoes provided did not have a protective toecap, lodge them as a production.[9]

---

[8] *Grace Shipping v. Sharp & Co.* 1987 Lloyds Law Reports 207 at page 15.
[9] See e.g. *English v North Lanarkshire Council*, 1999 Rep L.R. 53, where a dangerous meat slicing machine was brought to court.

Proof Preparation

Status of documentary evidence

In every civil proof there will be documents which you will wish to introduce in evidence. Always spend some preparation time considering how this will be done.

In the absence of any agreement, joint minute or notice to admit, you will need a witness to identify the document and its provenance. An expert witness is entitled to refer to documentation produced by him, and with which he is familiar by reason of his area of practice.

Otherwise where there are joint minutes or notices to admit, be very careful that you understand the precise extent of the agreement or admission.

- *An agreement that certain facts relevant to the case are true*
  This constitutes a judicial admission, and any contrary evidence to the point is inadmissible.

- *An agreement that documents are what they bear to be*
  This means that the documents are agreed as being authentic. It does not mean that they have been introduced in evidence, nor that they are evidence of their contents. If you want what is in the documents to be evidence in your case you will have to do more.

- *An agreement that documents are to be admitted as evidence of their contents*
  This means that you have agreed that the documents are authentic and can be considered by the court as evidence, but not that their contents must necessarily be accepted.

- *An agreement that documents are authentic and are admitted as true*
  These documents can be introduced as evidence and are conclusive of the facts which they contain.[10]

---

[10] See the discussion of these distinctions in *Lenaghan v. Ayrshire & Arran Health Board* 1994 S.C. 365.

Witness preparation

Imagine that you are at a party and someone asks you what you did on the very first day of your foreign holiday last year. The chances are that caught cold, you would struggle to remember this in any detail. But once you had time to think about it and to exercise your mind on the question, it is likely that the day's events would come flooding back. So prior to proof the pursuer should be prepped in the sense that he is forced to bring his best recollection to bear on the critical events. You should do this by arranging a pre-proof meeting with the pursuer.

Pre-proof meeting with the client

Set aside at least a couple of hours. Explain the court procedures to him. Carry out a dry run examination-in-chief. This is not principally for your benefit, but is a refresher exercise for the witness. Make sure that he has seen and can identify any documents or photographs. Anticipate the lines of cross-examination and put the substance to him. This is not the same as suggesting answers or otherwise seeking to trim his evidence, each of which constitutes professional misconduct. The distinction was elegantly made by Judge Francis Finch in *re. Eldridge* in 1880.[11]

> "While a discreet and prudent attorney may very properly ascertain from witnesses in advance of the trial what they in fact do know, and the extent and limitations of their memory as a guide for his own examinations, he has no right legal or moral, to go further. His duty is to extract the facts from the witness, not to pour them into him; to learn what the witness does know, not to teach him what he ought to know."

Explain how you will take the evidence from him. Tell him to respond politely when he is answering your opponent's questions, but not to volunteer any extra information. He should not become argumentative or rude. If he does not know the answer he should say so. The final admonition must be at all times to tell the truth. A particular point relates to a pursuer where there are other family members as witnesses. The pursuer will frequently be asked in cross-examination if there has

---

[11] *New York Court of Appeal* 37 NY 161171.
See also the Bar Standards Board "*Preparing Witness Statements for Use in Civil Proceedings*", 2008.

been any discussion, in an attempt to show either contamination of the evidence, or discrepant answers between witnesses. It is overwhelmingly likely that there has been some family discussion about the events, in which case the witness should say so. The issue is whether the evidence is substantially his own. Don't let him become confused or flustered by thinking he cannot answer this question truthfully. Finally a pursuer should be told to dress conservatively.

Preparation of other witnesses

Other witnesses should also be prepped. At the very least they should be refreshed with copies of their statements. They should not be confronted with documents or photographs for the first time in the witness box. So send any photographs or documents to them along with their citation. Ideally you should take at least a refresher telephone statement from the witness shortly prior to proof for the same recollection reasons described above.

The defenders' witness statements

There is no property in a witness. Over the past 100 years the Scottish courts have been unequivocal in upholding the right to precognosce witnesses for the opposing side. However it is a right which is easier to state than to enforce. Realistically you should do all you can to take statements from all the lay witnesses on the defender's list. Where there is an outright refusal at the very least you are entitled to rely on what is said in *Macphail's Sheriff Court Practice*, 3rd Edition at 15.08, namely that any such refusal is indicative of prejudice and partisanship. Lodge any correspondence relating to your requests.

2 APPEARING IN COURT - THE RULES AND RITUALS

"I have every confidence in the justice of my country," said Jack, smiling at the pompous sound of his words.
"Have you ever been present at a trial?" asked Stephen.
"Courts-martial by the score, but never a civilian trial. All mine have taken place when I was away at sea."
"I have listened to some, alas" said Stephen, "and I do assure you, brother, that the rules of the game, what constitutes evidence, the exits and entrances, and who is allowed to speak when, and what he may say, are infinitely more complex than they are in naval law. It is a game that has been going on for hundreds and hundreds of years, growing more tortuous with every generation, the rules multiplying, the precedents accumulating, equity interfering, statutes galore, and now it is such a black bitter tangle that a layman is perfectly helpless. I do beg you will attend to this eminent counsellor, and follow his advice."

>Patrick O'Brian *The Reverse of the Medal,* Harper Collins, 1986, an Aubrey-Maturin story. Jack is later wrongly convicted of stock market fraud.

Every day the courts where you practise make critical decisions with dramatic effects on the lives of their users. It is salutary to remind ourselves that historically litigation displaced other more robust forms of self-help. In "The Crisis of the Aristocracy 1558–1641" the historian Lawrence Stone ascribes the rise of common law litigation in 17th century England in part to the proscription of duelling. Our civil procedure is mainly adversarial, and feelings can and do run high from time to time. It is precisely because of this that adherence to the rules is vital. The rules and procedure are there to regulate, formalise and defuse what is an antagonistic process. So if at first the rituals of the sheriff court seem unduly stylised, you should remember what they are replacing. Civility and courtesy are great lubricants of

Appearing in Court – the Rules and Rituals

persuasion. G.K. Chesterton observed that people quarrel because they don't know how to argue. Your goal must always be to present the argument for your client in its strongest light without ever degenerating into a quarrel with your opponent no matter how provocative her behaviour.

Practical Points

1. **Introducing Yourself**

    Where you are appearing in a new court you should stand and introduce yourself and your opponent. If he is a solicitor or solicitor/advocate, he is your "friend". If counsel he is your "learned friend". Address the sheriff as "My lord" or "My lady". Some of the older books on advocacy advise that you should begin by saying "May it please the court My lord............." Although this is a time honoured incantation throughout the common law world, it is virtually meaningless and is rarely heard now in the sheriff court.

2. **Dress**

    In open court you will require to wear a gown, unless and until the sheriff tells you not to. Otherwise you may well hear a variation on the line "I can't hear you" as you attempt to address the court ungowned. If you are dealing with any matter in the sheriff's chambers there is generally no need for a gown. In that event it is customary to stand in chambers until invited to sit down. Your role as an advocate is best described as "invisible persuasion". The case is not about you. The advice must always be to dress conservatively according to the norms of the day. So men should keep the earring stud or other expressions of individual style for the weekend. Questions of dress are also subject to the practice rule formulated by Judge Judy. In her court the burden of proof was always on the guy in the polyester suit.

3. **Seating**

    The pursuer's agent will generally sit at the right hand side of the table facing the bench, with the defenders' agent to the left. You should get to your feet and stay standing whilst you are addressing the court. You may remain seated whilst the sheriff is speaking, but the advice is to stand in the event that any kind of exchange is taking place.

4. Attitude to the bench

A modern court is a place of business. Your job is to assist the sheriff by enabling him competently to analyse the facts and the law. Your duty is "zealous advocacy", and the system won't deliver justice unless you practise it.

> *"Solicitors must at all times do, and be seen to do, their best for the client and must be fearless in defending their client's interests, regardless of the consequences to themselves (including, if necessary, incurring the displeasure of the bench)."*[12]

So respect for judicial office does not translate into hand wringing obsequiousness. The legal world is not a community of saints. There is an element of rough and tumble. You will occasionally have to deal with brusqueness, discourtesy and even rudeness. Toughen up and get over it. Instances of judicial bullying are now thankfully rare. If you do find yourself being treated unfairly, breathe in deeply and count to ten before saying anything, then argue your position as calmly as possible. In extreme situations if a shorthand writer is present, ask that she makes a note. Otherwise pointedly ask a colleague to write down everything that is said. This should have a sobering effect for everyone.

If matters still become unduly personalised and you find yourself on the verge of saying something in open court you will regret, suggest to the sheriff that the discussion be continued in chambers.

5. Entering and leaving the court

If you are entering a court which is in session, it is customary to bow towards the bench. Similarly if you are leaving a court where other matters are to follow, you should bow as you go. You must stand as the sheriff arrives on the bench, and you should not sit down until she does. Stand again as the

---

[12] Solicitors (Scotland) (Standards of Conduct) Practice Rules 2008 Rule 3(3).

sheriff leaves the court. You should never leave a sheriff in court by herself, and should remain in court until a clerk of court or bar officer comes to usher her off the bench.

No chirping! Mobile phones should be off completely and any iPad set to silent.

6. **Behaviour in court**

It is particularly important that you keep quite still whilst the sheriff administers the oath or an affirmation to witnesses. Once the case commences there is no formal line of communication between you and your opponent. All of your remarks must be addressed to the bench. This does not mean that you cannot make the occasional whispered aside, particularly if you are trying to be helpful, for instance, "You can lead the witness on this topic". But don't ever argue a point directly with your opponent. Never interrupt except to make a concession. Keep completely still and silent whilst your opponent is talking. In particular do not display your contempt for her submissions by disdainful tosses of the head, *sotto voce* remarks to a colleague or snorts of amusement.

7. **Citation of authorities**

Reported cases should be cited in preference to the scotcourts internet transcript. Some cases are truncated e.g. Reparation Law Reports, in which case you might use the scotcourts version where it contains the relevant passage. Where the case is reported both in Session Cases and Scots Law Times, the Session Case report should be used. If you are citing an English authority to the court, you should use the Appeal Court reports wherever possible, the reason being that these decisions contain the arguments for both parties. There are some references to authority which you must make. The court is relying on you to produce all relevant authorities, and in particular any adverse authorities. The decision of a single judge in the Outer House is not binding on a sheriff, but the reality is that it is highly persuasive and you should always produce it. You must produce anything relevant from the House of Lords or the Supreme Court and from the Inner House. Their decisions are binding on both sheriffs and sheriffs principal.

The decision of the sheriff principal in the sheriffdom where you are appearing is binding. Decisions from sheriffs principal in other sheriffdoms are technically not binding but again are highly persuasive. English case law is not binding in the sheriff court but again will be highly persuasive particularly where the issue relates to a United Kingdom statute. Relevant decisions of the House of Lords or the Supreme Court in English cases, or the Privy Council in Commonwealth cases, should always be brought to the attention of the bench. It cannot be emphasised enough that the sheriff is relying on you and your opponent to provide the legal framework in which she will make her decision. If you fail to find and produce the relevant adverse authority and the sheriff is later successfully appealed, you will quite properly have found a judicial enemy for life. If on the other hand you transparently show fairness, thoroughness and attention to detail, the court will place its trust in you. You may well find as a result that you and your clients are the beneficiaries in ways you might not always perceive immediately.

8. **Relations with your opponent**

The need for courtesy and civility has already been noted. You may become friendly with some of the agents with whom you contend. In court keep your distance. Many members of the public already agree with George Bernard Shaw that all professions are a conspiracy against the laity. Watching you laugh and joke with your opponent at the court table will confirm those suspicions. No matter the provocation never let your verbal or written communication degenerate into personalised abuse. In negotiations follow the Latin maxim "*Suaviter in modo, fortiter in re*" ("Gentle in manner, firm in execution"). If you have been successful do not seek to grind your opponent into the dust. Metaphorically leave them their bus fare home. If you have lost, congratulate your opponent with as much good grace as you can muster. There will be another day, and you are in this career for the long run.

9. **Pre-proof checklist – the day before**

- Is there a certified record in process, incorporating any late amendments? If you are seeking a last minute amendment on the morning take a record incorporating the proposed amendment which you can tender.

Appearing in Court – the Rules and Rituals

- In an ordinary action has the shorthand writer been instructed?

- Are the productions in a properly numbered inventory, with a page number for each page? The numbering practice for inventories seems to vary from court to court. So you might have two inventories which run from 5/1 – 5/4, and 5/4 – 5/9 respectively. Alternatively this might read 5/1/1 – 5/1/4 and 5/2/1 – 5/2/5. The former is the correct format based on court of session practice, but don't get religious about it, and go with whatever the presiding sheriff wants.

- Have you lodged a second set of productions for the sheriff at least 48 hours before the proof in terms of O.C.R. 29.12, or S.C.R. 17.2?

- If the productions are voluminous, put the sheriff's copies in lever arch binders with dividers.

- Do you have a set of witness citations for each witness you want to call, including the pursuer?

- Do you have contact numbers including mobile telephone numbers for all witnesses?

- Are there specialties with regard to witnesses and in particular are there any child or vulnerable witness notices?

- Has any evidence been taken on commission, in which case is the transcript in process?

- Are there any joint minutes or notices to admit which should be dealt with at the start?

- Have you advised the sheriff clerk that the case will be proceeding?

10. **Pre-proof checklist - the morning of proof**

- Arrive at the court at least 45 minutes and preferably an hour before the starting time. Check via the court lists as to where, when and before whom your case will commence.

- Seek out and introduce yourself to your opponent. Tidy up any last minute process issues. Discuss any agreements on evidence, photographs, documents and the like.

- Check in at the courtroom. Befriend both the clerk of court and the bar officer (this is not optional!). Find out the running order from the clerk. Ask if there is a ready reckoner for court dimensions in the event that you might want a point of reference for distances.

- Check with the bar officer that all your productions are in place, are easily retrievable, and that there are copies for the sheriff. Tell the bar officer in which waiting room your witnesses are situated. Give the bar officer a copy of your witness list.

- Make contact with the shorthand writer and give her a copy record for her use.

- Meet with your client. Advise her of any developments. Make sure the client has seen all documents or photographs which may be put in examination-in-chief. Reassure her as to the court process.

- Meet with witnesses who are in attendance. Have them sequestered in a witness room. Speak to each one briefly, again making sure that any documents or photographs will not come as a surprise. Tell them not to discuss the case amongst themselves. Where experts are due to be in attendance by agreement, have their mobile telephone numbers easily available and contact them before the case commences to advise an approximate time when they will be called.

- Take five minutes by yourself, away from your client, away from your opponent and outwith the agent's room. Take some deep breaths as recommended by Bridget. Focus.

11. **Dealing with your witnesses after the proof has commenced**

    The traditional advice is to begin and end with your strongest witnesses. This is said to engage in your favour the twin engines of *Primacy* and *Recency*. So when a positive first impression is made, other evidence tends to be viewed in its light *(Primacy)*. Similarly you should finish with one of your more convincing witnesses *(Recency)*. In the real world you will almost always have to commence with your pursuer whatever your assessment. The exigencies of witness availability will rarely allow you the luxury of choosing where you finish, but wherever possible end on a strong note.

    Before the case commences have a final check to ensure that none of your witnesses are in the courtroom. An exception can arise for expert witnesses who may be entitled to hear the factual background, but you will require to ask the court's permission in advance. After you have commenced the evidence in chief, you are unable to communicate with that witness except through the formal questioning process. So if there is a break for lunch you cannot have any discussion with the witness. You cannot tell the witness that she is doing fine, or find out what she will answer if you pursue a specific line. You must also tell her not to discuss the case with anyone else. The same advice applies wherever there is any kind of adjournment.

    Witnesses who are giving evidence, or who have given evidence, should not be allowed to mingle with your other witnesses in the case. It is up to you to tell them not to discuss their evidence with any of the other witnesses. You can seek further instructions and details from the remaining witnesses, but in general terms and not on the specifics of the evidence which has gone before. So it is permissible in a case which has commenced for you to ask a witness who has still to give evidence if he can say which hand delivered the punch. It is improper to say to that person that witness X has said that the punch was thrown with the left hand, what does she think?

3 THE BASIC DYNAMICS OF ADVOCACY

"A man may be an able judge; he may be a learned judge; but I have never known a truly great judge whose heart was not in sympathy with the Junior Bar. No one whose career has not been a failure can look back to the day of small things and remember how feeble were his early steps, without feeling his heart warm for those who now stand where he once stood. I remember as if but yesterday the first time I appeared before a Court, and with pallid cheek and faltering tongue endeavoured to impress upon the mind of the judge what I supposed to be the law. The years that have passed have failed to efface from my memory the awful sensation of hearing the sound of my voice dying away, without an idea as to where the next word was to come from."

> Edward M. Paxson, *The Road to Success or Practical Hints to the Junior Bar*, 1888.

Peter (*advocate*) wants Julian (*judge*) to know the score of the football match which was played last Saturday. Peter knows the result, but he is not allowed to tell it to Julian directly. He is unable to offer his personal opinion on anything. Julian is not allowed to ask Peter directly. Instead, Peter brings Simone (*witness*) who was at the match, into the conversation. He takes from her that she was in attendance, and asks would she please tell us the score? She does so. It is immediately apparent that this is really a most awkward and cumbersome way of eliciting information. But the example does illustrate the basic dynamics of examination-in chief, and in particular the direction of information flow.

Peter is not asking the question to find out the answer. He knows the answer. It is Peter who is communicating the information to Julian through the medium of the witness Simone. He is making a presentation, not carrying out an investigation. So his ability to control the witness and the evidence is critical.

The Basic Dynamics of Advocacy

The format of questions

In examination-in-chief (otherwise direct examination) only open questions are allowed. This rule is subject to some exceptions which we will see, but important testimony should emanate from the witness and not from the advocate. The competent advocate must be able if need be to move the witness through the whole of her testimony, using only non leading questions. Open or non leading questions generally begin or contain the words "What? Who? When? Where? Why? How?"

Or questions are framed in terms such as:

Q.   Please tell the court................

Or,

Q.   Please describe..................

In contrast, a leading question either contains or suggests the answer, effectively turning the advocate into the witness as he seeks agreement with his various propositions. A simple example illustrates the difference.

> "We come on the Sloop John B
> My grandfather and me.
> Around Nassau town we did roam,
> Drinking all night,
> Got into a fight,
> Well I feel so broke up
> I wanna go home"

Examination-in-chief using non leading questions would be along the following lines:-

Q.   Please tell the court your name?
Q.   What is your occupation?
Q.   How long have you been an able seaman?
Q.   What does being an able seaman involve?

- Q. What trips have you been on recently?
- Q. On what ship?
- Q. How many crew members were there?
- Q. Were any related to you?
- Q. Where did the ship berth?
- Q. For how long?
- Q. What did the crew do whilst the ship was berthed in port?
- Q. How did you spend the evenings and nights?
- Q. What happened on these nights?
- Q. How do you feel about that?
- Q. What do you want to do now?

It is arguable that question – "Were any related to you?" is potentially leading, as it contains the suggestion that there might be relatives on board, but the question can be answered yes or no and any objection would be highly unlikely.

If you were to ask the witness the questions in leading format, it would be something as follows:

- Q. Your full name is Able Seaman Barrett Bonden?
- Q. You recently sailed on the Sloop John B, didn't you?
- Q. Wasn't your grandfather with you at the time?
- Q. The ship berthed at Nassau?
- Q. It remained there for at least a fortnight, didn't it?
- Q. Whilst in port the crew would roam round Nassau town, didn't they?
- Q. You went with them, didn't you?
- Q. I understand that you spent the evenings drinking, is that correct?
- Q. On one of those evenings you got into a fight, didn't you?
- Q. As a result you now feel depressed, don't you?
- Q. You really just want to go home, isn't that right?

As a matter of format, adding tags like "didn't you?", "wasn't it?" and "isn't that correct?" turns the statement into a question, but fundamentally you are making a series of statements with which you wish the witness to agree. If you watch seasoned practitioners they will routinely dispense with the tag and simply curl their voice upwards at the end of the sentence to signify a question.

The Basic Dynamics of Advocacy

Speaking in court

See what Bridget says about dealing with your nerves. School yourself to speak slowly and clearly. Don't refer to the pursuer as "my client" (with all its connotations of a paid retainer) and instead refer to him either as "the pursuer" or by his full name, for example, "Mr Aubrey". When bringing in a new witness say "The pursuer calls Mr Stephen Maturin". Be careful about ever telling a judge that if A is established she must find B. Instead *invite* the judge to find B. Be courteous and show humility in your dealings with everyone in the courtroom and not just the sheriff. Don't get ahead of the court emotionally. Some witnesses may forfeit the right to courtesy, but never start out an examination in that frame of mind. Begin by introducing yourself and your opponent. Show with reference, for instance, to a proposed joint minute that you are a person of competence.

Be sincere and respectful to all. Remember in particular that nothing is ever the fault of the sheriff clerk. Be scrupulous about any possible mis-statement. Show that you can be trusted. Be inclusive. Have the witness "tell us….." or "tell my lord……………."

Don't fall out with your opponent. Judges hate to have to deal with hostility between advocates. When your opponent is talking, don't shake your head or otherwise exhibit signs of scorn or contempt. If anything err on the side of flattery:

> "Not even my friend's undoubted forensic skills can conceal the threadbare nature of the evidence which he has brought."

Try not to raise your voice at the end of sentences. It makes you sound unsure, feeble and querulous. Instead if you want the statement to sound authoritative drop the pitch of your voice at the end of it, whilst maintaining volume. When dealing with witnesses you will almost always have to tell them

- to speak up

- to speak slowly.

The Basic Dynamics of Advocacy

It is simplest to begin your examination with that instruction rather than await the almost inevitable shrieval intervention. Tell the witness that you are not simply having a conversation with them, and that what they say will be noted and written down. You should stand at least 2-3 metres away from the witness box so that she will keep her voice up in answer to you.

Eye contact

Reading from a notepad is not advocacy. If you cannot look people in the eye, you will never persuade them of anything. This means looking at the sheriff when speaking to her, and looking at the witness when examining.

4 EXAMINATION-IN-CHIEF

"What was the precise truth of the affair? Nobody could say. Truth in its least elevated and humble sense, truth as detail, truth as times and numbers, truth arrived at by observation and deduction – this kind of truth left the scene earlier. Like Mr Singh, it absconded. Unlike Mr Singh, it did not re-appear."

Ian Jack, *Unsteady People* contained in
The Country Formerly Known as Great Britain,
Jonathan Cape, London 2010.

"Truth, when not sought after, rarely comes to light."

Oliver Wendell Holmes.

Cases are won and lost on the facts. Those which you want to present will not march into court by themselves. Your photographs and documents are already lodged. It is now your task through the voices of the witnesses to elicit testimony which is vivid, detailed and compelling, and which is inoculated against cross-examination.

The outline advocacy statement

You know from your outline submissions the evidence which you will need from this witness. You will recall that a necessary pre-proof exercise is to distill what this witness says into a single outline statement in large font and double spaced.

This is what you will examine from. You should not write out questions. Rather the Advocacy Statement will be a recital of the critical facts which, with a little practice, you will automatically transform into "Who?" "What?" "Where?" etc., type questions.

Examination-in-chief

So if your Advocacy Statement says as follows:

> By around 8.00 p.m. I was feeling ill.
> Initially I didn't want to bother the doctor.
> Things got worse, much worse.
> Eventually I telephoned NHS 24.
> They listened to my symptoms, and immediately said they would send out an emergency doctor.
> A lady doctor arrived at my house about 15 minutes later.

This becomes:

> Q. How did you feel that day?
> Q. What did you decide to do as a result?
> Q. How did you feel after that?
> Q. What did you then decide to do?
> Q. Whom did you speak to?
> Q. What did you tell them?
> Q. What did they say they would do?
> Q. How long did you wait?
> Q. Did anyone arrive at your house?
> Q. Who was it?

Witness control

We know that leading questions in examination-in-chief will be objected to, or even worse, evidence obtained from leading questions will be ultimately treated as of no value. So we cannot proffer the evidence ourselves. But because you cannot lead the witness does not mean you cannot guide him. You are looking to facilitate his evidence, not tender it yourself. The ability to control and direct the witness during examination-in-chief is what distinguishes the competent advocate from the novice.

Open ended and closed questioning in direct examination

You already know the difference between leading and non-leading questions. There is a further consideration for the kinds of non-leading questions which you will use in examination-in-chief, namely the distinction between open-ended and closed

Examination-in-chief

non-leading questions. An open-ended question calls for a wide-ranging and frequently narrative answer.

> Q. What happened next?

is the archetypal example.

Closed questions call for short, precise answers which enable you to elicit the details of the case.

They direct the witness to a specific facet of the factual context. So if you ask the witness:

> Q. How would you describe the condition of your car after the collision?

You are asking an open-ended question. You might get lucky and the witness might address the particular point you wish to make. If you sharpen the question by asking it in a closed format:

Q. What condition was the bumper in?

you will have a much better chance of hearing what you want. So, if you want to establish that the perpetrator had black hair don't ask,

> Q. Please describe for the court the physical appearance of Mr X?

Simply ask,

> Q. What colour of hair did he have?

Wherever possible avoid the completely open "What happened next?" type of question, or even worse "What, if anything, happened next?" This type of question surrenders complete control to the witness. He is given a totally free rein to answer without having any clue as to the direction in which you want him to travel. As often as not you will get a narrative answer which rambles some considerable way off the point. This leaves you to follow up with a further "And what happened next after that?" type question.

Examination-in-chief

The following are standard techniques which can be used to usher the witness towards the areas in which you wish him to testify.

The guidance techniques

1. **Transitioning**

    This means giving a signpost to the court and to the witness of the subject matter. It is commenced not by questioning, but by a statement to the court and to the witness, for example:

    > "Mr Hanrahan, I want to begin by asking you a few questions about your personal background."

Every time the subject matter of the direct examination is changed you should advertise the fact to the court and to the witness, saying, for instance:

> "Mr Hanrahan, I would now like to direct your attention to your work in the retail industry."

There is nothing objectionable about any of these formulations. They are not suggesting an answer, but are directing the witness to the topic. They also encourage you to think in terms of the structure of the examination. What this means is that each chapter of the direct examination is dealt with thoroughly before moving on to the next. When you do you will say something along the lines of:

> Mr Hanrahan, now let me ask you about ……..
> I now want to ask you about …………………
> I now want to direct your attention to…………
> Did there come a time when …………………?

These are indicators to the witness and to the court that you will be dealing with a discrete element, and the witness knows the area into which he is being funnelled.

Examination-in-chief

"Did there come a time when?" is a useful alternative to the "What happened next?" question.

You may want to establish that the witness has personally intervened in an assault which he came upon whilst walking home. You have taken from him his general direction of travel and the time he started his journey. Then ask:

Q. Did there come a time when something unusual happened..........?
Q. What was it?

2. **Looping**

This technique effectively echoes the answers you get:

Q. What time did you get up at?

A. **About 8.00 a.m. or so.**

Q. How did you feel at 8.00 a.m.?

A. **I felt ill.**

Q. When you felt ill what did you do?

A. **I phoned the doctor.**

Q. When you phoned the doctor what did he say?

A. **It was a lady doctor. She said she would come to the house.**

Q. Did the doctor come to the house?

The effect is to build a staircase of answers where the questioner is able to keep a firm control of the witness by pinning him down to a particular point from his previous answer.

3. The use of alternatives

This is a method which enables you to bring the witness to the point without necessarily suggesting the answer. Strictly it should only be used where there is only one of two alternative factual positions.

So:

Q. When you arrived was he conscious or unconscious?

is a proper question in that only one of the alternatives can be true. It would not be appropriate to ask the witness:

Q Was the car red or blue?

when the car could have been any number of colours.

There is an intermediate situation where the use of alternatives is routinely permitted. So for example:

Q. Was the car going fast or slow?

would generally not be objected to. The witness's answer would give the examiner a chance to refine matters further. The key in this kind of questioning is to offer the witness a legitimate choice. Use of a phrase such as "whether or not" can be particularly effective. So take the following:

1Q. Weren't you in Glasgow on 12th May 2012?

This is a leading question and will be objected to.

2Q. Were you in Glasgow on 12th May 2012?

Although this question may be answered yes or no, the answer to the question, namely the whereabouts of the witness, is contained within it, and it is a leading question.

Examination-in-chief

    3Q. Can you remember whether or not you were in Glasgow on 12th May 2012?

Technically this is also a leading question for the same reason, but it will almost always be allowed.

The only proper open question is:

    Q. Where were you on 12th May 2012?

This is the correct format, but if every question has to be asked in this manner the court is in for a very long day.

You will hardly ever get an objection to a question in form 3. If you did you might legitimately suggest that the question is capable of a yes or no answer and that there is no deliberate attempt to influence the witness one way or another.

You shouldn't worry about the occasional objection. You are not going to lose the case because of a single leading question. If you don't get an objection from time to time, you are probably not controlling the witness properly. Once you start thinking about offering choices and using this kind of phrase you can utilise it all the time.

    Q. Was it a week day or a weekend?
    Q. Was it before noon or after noon?
    Q. Did you see the accused approach the witness or not?
    Q. Was the light red, amber or green?

Where an assault has been established:

    Q. Did he strike with his left hand or his right hand?
    Q. Was his hand open or was it closed to form a fist?

You can use questions which include every possibility:

    Q. Was the officer slim or fat or somewhere in between?

4. Use of context

Sometimes you know the answer you want, but can't seem to articulate the question in an open format. One solution is to give the witness a contextual clue by using a phrase such as

> In relation to........., or
> With regard to.........

So in the example below you want to elicit from the witness that when he joined the army as a medical officer, he was issued with an army revolver.

> Q. When did you join the army?
> Q. What was your rank?
> Q. In relation to military equipment, what was the standard issue to medical personnel?

The use of "with regard to", "in respect of", "in relation to" gives the witness a clue as to the direction of travel.

A further useful technique is to use "if any" phraseology if you are concerned that you are leading the witness. So in the above example you might ask:

> Q. What, if any, military equipment were you issued with?

5. What happened next?

There will be occasions when you are on your feet and your mind simply refuses to formulate the next question, except in those terms. When this happens, make the question as specific as possible by anchoring it in time and place. So, for example,

> Q. You told us that you entered the front door of the house, what happened immediately after that?

Examination-in-chief

6. Extract the specifics from the evidence

Suppose you want to persuade the court that the pursuer's vehicle was damaged beyond repair. If you ask the witness about its condition, you will likely hear:

    A.   It was very badly damaged

or

    A.   It looked terrible

and the like.

These descriptions contain a large element of subjectivity which are of little value to the court. You need to bring out the particulars, in an objective sense. So deploy questions such as:

    Q.   What condition was the steering column in?

    Q.   Describe the condition of the front passenger door?

or

    Q.   How was the bumper affected?

This gives the court a chance to make up a list of specifics justifying the pursuer's individual assessment.
Similarly if you ask a pursuer:

    Q.   How painful was your hand following your injury?

you are going to get answers ranging from "Extremely" to "Not very much after a while".

Instead ask the witness:

    Q.   I now want to ask you about the levels of pain you suffered as a result of your accident. (*Transition*).

Q. Can I direct your attention first of all to the three month period immediately following your accident?
(*Transition*)

Q. On a scale of one to ten with ten being the worst pain you have ever experienced, how would you describe that pain during those first three months?

5 THE ORGANISATION OF THE EXAMINATION-IN-CHIEF

"It may be my fault that I cannot follow you; I know that my brain is getting more dilapidated; but I would like to stipulate for some sort of order. There are plenty of them. There is the chronological, the botanical, the metaphysical, the geographical – even the alphabetical order would be better than no order at all."

Mr Justice Maule quoted in *First Steps in Advocacy*,
Leo Page, Faber and Faber, 1943.

You must structure this in advance. In a breach of contract case your order might be:

- Personal background of witness and relationship with other parties.
- Negotiation and formation of contract, oral or written.
- Terms of contract.
- Actions which constitute breach by other party.
- Notification of breach.
- Calculation of damages.

In a typical accident claim, your order would be:

- Personal background.
- General scene setting.
- Critical action in strict time order.
- Medical and damages evidence.

The Organisation of the Examination-in-chief

You should move the examination through this structure, alerting the sheriff where you are at each particular stage, using Transitions.

Introducing witnesses

Every time a person enters the witness box the court asks itself:

"Who is this person and why should she be believed?"

Blatant evidence as to good character is generally inadmissible but you are entitled to inform the court of the witness's general background and place in society. You want the sheriff to think that this is a person she can trust.

So always begin by obtaining from the witness her full name, age, marital or relationship status and family and employment details. Do this using open questions to enable the witness to familiarise herself with speaking in court.

In the accident claim example you would begin:

Q. I want to ask you briefly about your personal background.
Q. Are you in employment?
Q. What is your job?
Q. How long have you worked there?
Q. Do you have a husband or partner?
Q. How long have you been in this relationship?
Q. Do you have any children?

Deal with the witness's motivation for truth telling by establishing their independence, or alternatively immediately acknowledging a relationship.

> Q. Do you know the pursuer, Sophie Aubrey?
> A. **No.**
> Q. How is it that you come to give evidence in this case?
> A. **I saw a newspaper advert calling for witnesses to a road traffic accident involving a child on Garscube Road and I phoned the number**

The Organisation of the Examination-in-chief

Or alternatively,

> Q. What is your relationship to the pursuer?
> **A. We have been living together since 2009.**
> Q. Did something unusual happen to him in May of last year?
> **A. Yes, he was involved in an accident at work.**
> Q. How do you know about that?

Occasionally the material is less useful. In that event use leading questions to introduce the witness, for example:

> Q. Mr Jones, you appear today from custody?
> Q. You were sentenced in September 2012 to 6 months in jail for benefits fraud?
> Q. Was this was your first offence?

before moving quickly into any elements, for instance, independence, which might bolster credibility:

> Q. Do you have any connection with the pursuer?
> Q. Before his accident in 2012 had you ever met him?
> Q. Have you seen him at all since then?

Scene setting

Use a transitional phrase such as:
"I now want to direct your attention to your job at the Hallsworth factory."

Q. How big was the factory?
Q. How many people worked there?
Q. What did the factory produce?
Q. What raw materials were used?
Q. How were these delivered?
Q. How were the finished items despatched?

So you have a bird's eye view of the process before zooming in to take the details:

Q. What was your role in this process?
Q. Where was your workstation?
Q. What were your particular duties?
Q. How many people were in your team? Etc.

Use of photographs in examination-in-chief

Seeing is not only believing, it is also explaining. Try this out for yourself. Read the Inner House judgement in *Kennedy v. Chivas Brothers Ltd*,[13] a manual handling case involving the use of a mobile trolley. The court has taken the unusual step of incorporating actual photographs in the appeal judgement. Think of how difficult it would be to understand the factual nuances of the judgement simply from a written text, and how clear matters are as a result of the photographs. Wherever possible augment your proof with visual aids.

There is a school of thought which says that you can get the most out of photographic evidence by having the witness describe the scene in his own words first of all, and only later by referring to the photographs. In this way you effectively get the benefit of the evidence twice. This might work for e.g. a simple road traffic accident scene. However anything remotely complicated will be beyond the descriptive skills of most witnesses and will simply lead to delay, confusion and shrieval annoyance. It is much simpler to take the witness directly to the photographs. Ideally you should have these agreed by joint minute or notice to admit that, for example:

> "The photographs Nos 5/4 (a-e) of process are what they bear to be, were taken by Patrick O'Brian on 3rd May 2013, and the photographs are admitted as evidence in the cause."

If there is some genuine dispute as to the authenticity of the photographs, you will have to bring the photographer as a witness. In most cases it will not be necessary to set up the photographs in either of the above ways, as long as the witness can confirm that they correspond with the scene.

I am now going to show you some photographs.
Q. Can you look at 5/1 of Process?

---

[13] [2013] CSIH 57

The Organisation of the Examination-in-chief

> Q. Can you tell us what 5/1 shows?
> Q. Can you say whether or not that was the scene generally when you worked for the defenders?
> Q. What if any difference is there?
> Q. Please hold up the photograph so that everyone in the court can see it. Now please point to the area which shows your work station.
> Q. You have pointed to an area on the bottom right hand side looking at the photograph next to a single desk where there is a computer.

You have translated the witness's action into a verbal summary. This is important because this description will have to be comprehensible in the shorthand notes.

The critical action

Use a transitional phrase such as:

> I now want to turn to the events of 30th July 2012. (*Transition*)

Take these slowly. Looping is helpful in this area. It is particularly useful when you want to exert some form of control over the witness by moving through the chronology of the accident, without resorting to leading questions.

Avoid wind-ups

Don't give your witness the opportunity to be vague or indecisive. So don't say to her:

> Q. Can you recall the weather conditions on 20th May this year?

But ask:

> Q. What was the weather like on 20th May this year?

Also avoid the escape route frequently handed to witnesses by use of a tag added to a question along the lines of:
"………………………..if you can't remember just say so."

Demonstrating distances

For small distances ask the witness to stretch out his arms to his estimate of the length. You now have to get this into the notes. Ask the court if it can be agreed that the distance is about e.g. a metre. Your opponent will generally concede the point. Summarise by saying:

> "It should be noted that the witness is extending his arms by about a metre or so."

For greater distances use the dimensions of the courtroom.

> Q. I now want to ask how far away you were when you saw the collision? *(Transition)*
> Q. Please compare that distance to the distance from where you are to the courtroom door.
> **A. I would say it's about the same.**
> Q. Well we know that distance is 8 metres. Is that about right?

Interrupting your own witness

If a garrulous witness obviously goes off the topic and starts to give some lengthy and irrelevant narrative, you can stop him mid-flow –

"Thanks for that Mr Bonden, but I now want to direct you specifically to the actual tool you were using on the accident date." *(Transition)*.

> Q. Do you know who manufactured it?

Dealing with bad facts

Every child who hears the admonition "Wait until your mother/father gets home", knows instinctively that if he wants to minimise punishment, he must get his version in first. In the same way the sheriff must hear of any problems in the case from you.

If there is bad news in the case, (and there is almost always some), you must be its bearer. The temptation is always to ignore the difficulties in the hope that your

The Organisation of the Examination-in-chief

opponent will do so also. Resist. Face up to them, and do your best to inoculate the witness against the inevitable cross-examination to follow.

So, for example,

- Q. After this incident how long did you carry on working for the defenders in the supermarket?
- Q. Why did that employment come to an end?
- A. **I was dismissed.**
- Q. What happened?
- A. **I took home some tins of fruit for my own use.**
- Q. How many did you take?
- Q. Why did you do that?
- A. **The tins were damaged and I didn't think anyone would mind.**
- Q. Do you now accept that this is theft?
- Q. Has anything like that ever happened to you in any other employment?
- Q. How long have you been in your present job as a picker?

Refreshing the memory of a witness

A typical scenario is where a police officer has no actual recollection of the event, but has made an entry in his notebook. However, the procedure is not limited to police witnesses and will apply to any person who by the time of the proof cannot remember the event, but composed a contemporaneous note or report. You must first of all ask the witness to exhaust his memory:

- Q. Constable Stone, on 21st August last year you attended at a road traffic accident at Garscube Road? (*leading, but attendance is not in dispute*).
- A. Yes.
- Q. What if any steps did you take to interview the drivers involved?
- A. **I am afraid I can't remember exactly what I did that day.**
- Q. Did you have your police notebook with you?
- Q. Did you note what was said to you at the time?
- Q. Do you have the notebook with you now?
- Q. Please look at the notebook. Does that refresh your memory as to what you were told by Mr Green?
- A. **He said he hadn't seen the other car because he was blinded by the sun.**

The notebook does not become a production, although it should be made available to your opponent (but not the sheriff) during the examination of the witness.[14]

Re-examination

At the end of the cross-examination you have an opportunity to revisit areas where inroads have been made into the evidence in chief. This is an extremely difficult skill. You are still limited to non-leading questions. You run the risk of the witness making matters worse. So don't re-examine at all unless you have to. However you may be clear that some concessions were made which do not reflect the witnesses' true position. Where you want to re-examine direct the witness to the passage by a Transition introduction such as:

> Q. You told my friend you had some discussion with your sister about the matter. It might be suggested that what you told the court earlier in this case was not your own recollection but that of your sister. *(Transition).* Please tell the court whether the evidence you gave earlier today is your own recollection or not?
> Q. To what extent has it been influenced by the discussions you had with your sister?

You are not allowed to re-open areas which were not the subject of cross-examination. So if you have forgotten to explore the issue in evidence in chief you cannot resurrect it in re-examination, unless there has been some reference to it in cross. If you find that you have forgotten to ask about something fundamental you should apologise and ask that the question is put to the witness by the court. (See below).

Questioning by the court

At the end of re-examination very frequently the sheriff will have questions for the witness. These are a direct window into her thinking, and should be noted carefully. It ill becomes the judge to become an advocate for either side and you can properly object to any line of questioning which goes beyond basic factual inquiry to clear up ambiguities.[15] After the sheriff is finished she will generally invite each side to

---

[14] *Hinshelwood v. Auld* 1926 J.C. 4
[15] *Nisbet v. H.M. Advocate* 1979 SLT (Notes) 5.

The Organisation of the Examination-in-chief

ask any questions arising from what has just been said. The same rules as to re-examination apply. Don't ask anything unless you are very sure that the witness will clear matters up as opposed to making things worse.

6 CROSS-EXAMINATION

"At 12.15 on the morning of March 18 [1946] Mr Justice Jackson rose to begin the long-awaited cross-examination [of Hermann Goering]. The Court filled quickly as the House of Commons fills when a speech of great importance is to be made.........., but before the adjournment had been reached it was clear that all the high hopes were to be disappointed, and that so far from the cross-examination destroying the Nazi case, it was to be the means whereby the Defendants in the dock were to be stimulated and encouraged..........to explain and expound their ideas and beliefs for future generations of Germans.

..........The cross-examination had not proceeded more than ten minutes before it was seen that he [Goering] was the complete master of Mr Justice Jackson...... Mr Justice Jackson, despite his great abilities and charm and his great powers of exposition had never learnt the very first elements of cross-examination....... He was overwhelmed by his documents, and there was no chance of the lightning question following upon some careless or damaging answer, no quick parry and thrust, no leading the witness onto the prepared pitfall, and above all no clear over-riding conception of the great issues which could have been put with simplicity and power."

>   *The Diaries of Lord Birkett KC, Justice at Nuremberg,*
>   pps 509-511.

Mr Justice Jackson had been a member of the American Supreme Court since 1941. His cross-examination of Goering has been universally acknowledged as a disastrous failure.

I have seen eminent advocates carry out unsuccessful cross-examinations and have conducted many unsuccessful cross-examinations myself. Most involve lack of planning and unrealistic ambitions for the cross. Witnesses who will give it up under your penetrating gaze exist only in screenplays like "My Cousin Vinny" where it is written into the script. Unsuccessful cross-examinations tend to be characterised by basic errors of approach as follows:

1. The lawyer as supplicant

The cross begins with an obsequious exchange of pleasantries. It develops into a series of begging requests along the lines of "Are you sure you're sure?" If anything the witness becomes even surer during the course of the examination. All that has been achieved is a reinforcement of the evidence in chief.

2. The lawyer as bully

The lawyer adopts a hostile and hectoring tone right from the start. It is not so much cross-examination as examining crossly. The problem with this approach is that in most cases at the outset of the cross-examination the judicial sympathy will be with the witness. The lawyer may have some ammunition with which to attack the witness, but uses it too quickly, misses the chance of obtaining any kind of concessions, and gets ahead of the court emotionally. The cross-examination frequently degenerates into an argument with the lawyer typically insisting on Yes/No answers, or even worse getting involved in a dialogue with the witness.

3. The lawyer as explorer

The lawyer travels hopefully, traversing areas where he has no real idea of the likely responses, and no prepared riposte in the event of difficulties. You should always proceed on the assumption that the witness will hurt you if he can. Even a completely unbiased and independent witness with no axe to grind tends to have an attachment to his own version of the facts. If this version was helpful, you would be calling him and would be examining in chief. What you should have is a safe area or areas where you have some material with which you can control or even discredit the evidence. Think of this area as a gated compound in the middle of a hostile jungle. Do not leave the compound. You will be cut to pieces.

The fundamentals

You are required to put your client's version of events to at least some of the opposing witnesses. Whilst failure to do so does not necessarily lead to the contrary evidence being accepted, it is a significant hurdle to overcome if you fail to allow the witnesses to comment. The basic tool of cross-examination is the leading question. Use of the leading question enables you to argue your client's case to the opposing witness. Avoid the hoary circumlocution "I put it to you……" and instead make a series of statements turned into a question by either a "didn't you" type tag, or a raised questioning voice.

Cross-examination proceeds under the so called "English rule" whereby the topics in cross are not limited to subjects raised in examination-in-chief. Ethically you must have some kind of material to justify the cross-examination. So for example in a road traffic case it might be legitimate to suggest to the defender that he was in a hurry to get home. It would be quite improper without some materials in your papers to suggest to him that he was under the influence of alcohol at the time.

Otherwise you are able to explore, probe and contradict as you see fit.

Remember that although you are generally free to roam at large, your opponent is entitled to re-examine on the areas which you raise. Areas of evidence which might otherwise be inadmissible or simply forgotten about can be admitted via re-examination, if you are unwise enough to stray there during cross.

Note taking

All cross-examination should be planned in advance with topic matters, but you will rarely if ever follow the plan slavishly. Do not waste your time during examination-in-chief by attempting to note every word which the witness says. Instead watch the witness carefully, let him know you are watching him, and note any answers where he appears hesitant or unsure. Generally there will be a few points on which you must cross examine. Take a note of these as you go along. Methods of note taking vary. Some advocates divide the page into two, with questions on the left hand side and answers on the right. This may work for you, but it produces a lot of writing and not enough thinking. It is much better simply

Cross-examination

to note the important answers (not the questions) and to integrate these into your pre-planned cross.

After listening to the examination-in-chief the first decision you have to make is whether you have to cross examine at all. If the witness hasn't harmed you, simply stand up and say dismissively "No cross-examination". The advocacy literature abounds with war stories about unfortunates who have ignored this rule. I suspect most are apocryphal. Perhaps the best relates to the US criminal defence of two women charged with running a brothel, masquerading as a health club. The prosecution led evidence from a pizza delivery worker who in chief would only say that whenever he delivered the pizza there were lots of girls around. Counsel for the first accused declined the opportunity to cross examine. Unable to leave well alone, the inexperienced counsel for the second accused could not resist asking:

> Q. So in all your visits there you never saw anything unusual or untoward?

to be met with a reflective pause, and then the answer:

> **A.** I did once see a naked man on a dog leash.[16]

Order and pace of cross-examination

The order of cross-examination is important, as is the pace. Keep things moving along briskly. Do not alert the witness in advance to the direction of your questioning. You will not be using signposts or transitions because the objective is to wrong foot, and to give him as little thinking time as possible. You will frequently want to commit him to a position on which you have material to undermine and confront. The pace of the cross will generally be dictated by the sheriff who has to note the answers, but long pauses between questions help the witness and hinder the cross-examiner. This does not mean that the cross should be disordered, only that you should not be signposting.

---

[16] This is taken from a highly entertaining compilation *Your Witness: Lessons on Cross-examination and Life from Great Chicago Trial Lawyers* edited by Steven F. Molo and James R. Figliulo, Law Bulletin Publishing Company, 2008.

Cross-examination

1. Control the witness

The single most important part of your preparation is the ingathering of all possible material with which you can exert some control over the witness. So everything that the witness has previously said on the subject should be collected rigorously. This might be what was said at a medical examination, or what was said to a police officer, or what was said in an email. Material which a witness has signed or is in his own handwriting can be used to devastating effect. (See the later section on prior inconsistent statements). Ideally every cross-examination should be short and pointed. Treat each question as if it were personally costing you £100.00. Every exchange in cross-examination is a skirmish with the witness which you will either win or lose. The only weapons you have to control the witness are:

- the use of leading questions;
- prior inconsistent statements;
- the laws of probability.

2. Stick to one fact per question

If you ask the question:

> Q. You were in Dumbarton last Sunday at about 5.00 p.m. with Andrew and Myra Ward outside the cinema, weren't you?"

you have given the witness all kinds of quibble and wriggle room. Instead take it point by point:

> Q. You were in Dumbarton last Sunday, weren't you?
> Q. At about 5.00 p.m. that day you were with Andrew and Myra Ward, weren't you?
> Q. You were standing outside the cinema at that time?

and pin the witness down stage by stage.

3. Have a plan for each witness you will cross-examine

Formulate realistic ambitions for each cross-examination and plan your tactics accordingly. You will only rarely have the material to knock down the witness completely. Remember that in cross-examination it is not what the witness says, it is whether he is believed. Your aim should be to sideline what he is saying by reference to motivation, opportunity for observation, previous inconsistent statements, documentary and other witness evidence, and the general rules of probability. With regard to the latter, for example:

> Q. Mr Kelly, you had sight of the person who bought the clothing for a few minutes at the most?
> Q. You were about 10 metres away from him, weren't you?
> Q. Mr Kelly have you ever seen a friend across the street and you decided to go to speak with him and when you got there you discovered that it wasn't your friend at all?
> Q. That kind of thing happens to everyone doesn't it?

4. Hitch-hike for concessions first

In almost all cases you should be able to extract some evidence which is favourable to your client or where matters are essentially in agreement. Witnesses are at their most cooperative towards the start of each cross-examination. It is at this time that you should elicit favourable testimony, even if only on non-contentious matters. This will prove much more difficult if you immediately launch into a hostile cross-examination on areas where you feel you must cross-examine.

So you might ask:

> Q. Can we agree that X has an exemplary sickness record?

Wherever possible rack up the points of agreement before attempting to undermine or confront an adverse witness.

5. Make eye contact and listen to the answers

This is easily the most difficult but the most important aspect of cross-examination. Bridget has a listening exercise which will improve your listening skills and help you pay attention to what is actually said to the end of the sentence. Cross-examination with your head down in your notepad does not work. You must have an outline plan, and an idea of prepared questions, but you must be ready to adapt or even abandon these depending on the actual answers you receive. You cannot control a witness from a script. You must always be alert to nuances, voice mannerisms and gesture which indicate vulnerable points in the testimony, and be prepared to pounce. You cannot create a dynamic of cross-examination if you are continually losing eye contact by referring to your notes or fumbling amongst your papers for documentary productions.

You will occasionally come across a witness who is so amenable that he or she agrees with almost everything that you put. Whilst you may think the cross is going swimmingly, you should know that he or she will be equally suggestible on re-examination. However the re-examiner cannot use leading questions. This makes it especially important where you have made some progress with the witness to be on your mettle to object to leading questions in re-examination. The temptation for the re-examiner to begin by asking:

> Q. Is it not the case that………..?

or

> Q. Would you agree with me that ……..……?

seems almost irresistible. You must object or you will see all your good work crumble to dust.

6. Insist on an answer

This is the corollary to listening to the witness. You will frequently get a non-responsive answer, often at some length. Remind the court and the witness of the question, repeat it, and insist that the witness answer.

Cross-examination

7. Insisting on a yes/no answer?

The only time you should use this technique is if the witness prevaricates and evades the point of the question. So your question is answered or part-answered, but the witness wants to add on an explanatory tag. Repeat the question and insist that the witness answer yes or no. Cut off any attempted further explanation. Tell the witness that the other lawyer will have the opportunity to clear up any ambiguities. Otherwise insistence on Yes/No with a witness who is doing his best seems a bit of a lawyer's trick, so don't employ it without good cause.

8. The witness answers with a question

> Q. You didn't wait for the police to arrive, did you?

> A. **Yes of course I left the scene of the accident. No one was hurt. I had to rush home to look after my children. What would you have done?**

Don't tell the witness what you would have done. Explain that you are not allowed to answer, that your role is limited to asking questions, and that her role is to answer them. Try not to sound too pompous or lawyerly as you do so. The impression should be that you would love to enter into a dialogue with the witness but unfortunately can't, when of course the last thing you want to do is to have to deal with the point of the witness's question.

9. Pitting of one witness against another

In the sheriff court you frequently hear questions along the lines of

> Q. If Mrs Maturin were to give evidence later that you weren't there at the time of the accident, she must be mistaken, mustn't she?

Some sheriffs will sustain an objection to this kind of question. They take the view that the witness is there to answer questions of fact, not to speculate on what Mrs Maturin might or might not say. So it is probably improper to put prior or expected testimony to the witness and ask for a comment on it. It is acceptable to explore any motivation known to the witness being examined. So whilst putting the contents of the expected testimony might not be appropriate, it is permissible and helpful to ask questions along the lines of

Q. Mrs Maturin is known to you isn't she?
Q. Do you know of any motive she might have to provide evidence against you in this matter?

10. The independent percipient witness; have realistic ambitions

You are not going to knock down this witness. You might undermine him.

Q. You were some distance away?
Q. The lighting was poor wasn't it?
Q. You were looking in the shop window?
Q. Your attention was first drawn to the scene by a bang which you heard?
Q. You didn't see any of the vehicles beforehand?

Avoid the temptation to ask the ultimate question.

Q. So why are you now able to estimate the speed of the blue car?

The witness will probably tell you precisely why. You have made your point before the last question, and the chances are that you will get an answer which undoes all your previous progress. Of course it is open to the examiner-in-chief to re-examine but he cannot use leading questions. In any event your questions have been for the benefit of the sheriff. You have given him an opportunity to sideline the evidence of the witness if he wants to.

11. Confronting the witness

You should only use this if you have the kind of material which we previously discussed. The order of taking the evidence is critically important. You must first of all have the witness re-commit to his evidence-in-chief. Having walked him up the garden path you then close the gate firmly behind him by having him confirm that he is certain about the evidence he has just given. Once you have done so you can then confront the witness. So by way of example:

Cross-examination

> Q. You have just told the court that you had a clear view of the collision?
> Q. Following the accident you were interviewed by P.C. Gibson, weren't you?
> Q. You told her that you hadn't seen what happened, didn't you?

12. Use of prior inconsistent statements

You cannot put precognitions to witnesses, but you can put previous inconsistent statements such as material which they have signed or where for example you have a handwritten version. You should first of all decide what you are trying to achieve.

a. Do you want to argue that the first version was correct? For example in an accident case do you want to say that the witness is basically credible but is more likely to have told the truth the closer in time to the event? In that case you want the first version to be accepted, or do you want to argue:

b. That the witness is not at all credible or trustworthy and that no version should be accepted.

There are generally three steps.

Step 1 – Recommittal

Tell the witness what his evidence was in the form of a leading question:

> Q. Mr Banks, you just told the court that you were in the reprographic room when the explosion occurred?

Step 2 – Validate the previous version

> Q. Mr Banks, this accident was investigated by the Health & Safety Executive. Do you remember that?
> Q. It was investigated by Mr Hargreaves of the Health & Safety Executive wasn't it?
> Q. In fact, Mr Hargreaves interviewed a number of employees. Isn't that right?

Cross-examination

    Q.   You were one of them?
    Q.   You knew how important the investigation was didn't you?
    Q.   Mr Hargreaves spoke to you about the incident didn't he?
    Q.   This was only a few days after the explosion?

Step 3 – Confront the witness with the previous version

    Q.   Can I ask you to look at 5/7 of Process?
    Q.   It is a record of the HSE investigation. Do you see that?
    Q.   There is a statement by you there.
    Q.   That is your signature isn't it?
    Q.   It is recorded there at ……………………..

You read aloud the extract to the witness –

    Q.   That is what you have signed for.
    Q.   You weren't in the Reprographic Room, were you?
    Q.   You were in the Moulding Room at the time, weren't you?

Don't ask the witness to read from the extract, but do it yourself. Otherwise you give him time to re-assess the situation and come up with obfuscations. Never ask the witness to explain. This will inevitably elicit some self-serving explanation as to why his evidence in court is now to be preferred over his previous testimony.

13. Lines of cross-examination

One useful planning method is to think of what the ideal evidence for the other side would be from this witness and concentrate on the areas in which it is lacking. So, for example, you have a witness who says that an accident did not occur while he was present. His ideal evidence would be to the effect that some other occurrence which he learned about happened at a different time, and this explains the pursuer's absence from work. In his evidence he gives no explanation and has no curiosity whatsoever about why the pursuer was absent. Your cross would proceed along the lines of:

Cross-examination

>Q. Your colleague did not appear for work that afternoon?
>Q. She did not appear for three or four weeks afterwards?
>Q. You didn't know why she was off work?
>Q. You didn't ask anyone why she was off?
>Q. You were told in fact that she had had an accident at work?

14. Prior discussions

>Q. Have you discussed this case with the defender?

Although this is an open question there is almost no right answer. As previously observed witnesses sometimes think they are unable to answer this truthfully. They will answer no, leaving you to suggest that this is unlikely. When the answer is yes, this provides an opportunity to argue that the evidence of one has influenced the other.

15. Distance in time from the event

>Q. Your name appeared on the witness list in July of this year.
>Q. That was when that you were contacted by the defender's solicitors?
>Q. That was the first time you had been asked to think about these events since they happened almost 2 years ago?

7 OBJECTIONS

"In court he rarely raised objections when opposing counsel introduced evidence. He would say he reckoned it would be fair to let this in, or that, and sometimes when his adversary could not quite prove what Lincoln knew to be the truth, he reckoned it would be fair to admit the truth to be so-and-so. He never yielded essentials. What he was so blandly giving away was what he couldn't get and keep"

David Donald, *Lincoln*, at p.150,
Simon and Schuster, 1995

There are two major rules about objections.

1. Don't object unless you have to

There is a school of thought that says you should take every conceivable point of objection. The thinking is that it interrupts the flow of evidence, unsettles the witness, and generally puts your opponent off his stride. In reality there is nothing more annoying for a sheriff than to have the testimony continually disrupted with the witness frequently being told to wait outside, time wasted on arguments about admissibility and finally a requirement to pronounce as to whether to allow the line, refuse it, or have it heard under reservation. Don't object on points which are not crucial to your final argument. Lawyers everywhere might do well to emulate the trial technique of Abraham Lincoln as above.

Don't object if your opponent leads the witness on introductory material, on issues where there is general agreement, and on non-contentious background facts which you don't know to be true but don't really matter. Apart from anything else, a factual witness who has been spoon fed leading questions might well find it disconcerting suddenly to have to switch to open questions on the critical matters in dispute. You might agree with your opponent in advance that you won't object to the witness being led up to a certain point. Tell the court your position after the witness has been sworn and introduced to the court. You are saving everyone time and trouble and the court will appreciate it.

2. If you have to object do it right away

The general rule is that once evidence has been heard, it is available for consideration by the court, as long as the pleadings cover it.[17] So you may find any number of authorities after the fact which suggest that the evidence should not have been allowed. Unless you have objected timeously the evidence is in.

Evidence which has been objected to is frequently heard "Under reservation as to its competency and relevancy".

Where you know that the same point is going to be made through the mouths of several witnesses, it is acceptable to put down a "running objection" marker when the testimony first emerges.[18]

Prudence dictates that you should unobtrusively remind the court each time the point arises of new. School yourself to be on alert for the objectionable question which requires your immediate interjection. As you will see, particularly for leading questions, there is a common phraseology which should galvanise you each time you hear the framework commenced.

Can you object to an answer as opposed to a question? If you have dozed through the question and half of the answer, the sheriff is likely to tell you that your objection comes too late and that you can't object to an answer, only to a question. But that is not quite the whole truth. You can object to a "non-responsive" answer, that is where the witness does not answer the question posed, but instead takes the opportunity for a self-serving piece of evidence otherwise inadmissible.

As ever preparation is the key. Other than leading questions, which can arise in any circumstances, the evidential pressure points should be obvious. You will have anticipated that your opponent might try to introduce character evidence, evidence of collateral facts, or try to provide evidence for a case not on record. You should have your arguments and authorities ready.

---

[17] *McGlone v. British Railways Board,* 1966 SC HL(1).
[18] *Hyslop v. Lynx Express Parcels,* 2003 SLT 785.

Objections

Dealing with objections

The sheriff may pronounce immediately, for example, by warning your opponent to stop leading the witness. But in any matter of import, the likely outcome is that the evidence will be heard under reservation. This is mandatory in a summary cause (S.C.R 8.15). In an ordinary action any submissions made at the time should be noted by the shorthand writer. (OCR 29.18(5)). The question of admissibility should then be dealt with at final submissions and the judgement should deal with the arguments. As many commentators point out, the bell cannot be un-rung. However the theory is that a sheriff, as opposed to a jury, is able to put the excluded evidence completely from his mind. The other dilemma is where you believe that there might be something in your opponent's submission, and that the evidence objected to is truly of critical importance to your case. The answer must always be to seek a brief adjournment to consider the point, and if necessary to compose a handwritten minute of amendment there and then. The court does not want to decide important matters on pleadings or technical issues. Everything will depend on the nature of your amendment, the timing of it and whether it involves real investigatory prejudice to the others side. The allowance of a minute of amendment is a matter of discretion in every case. You might expect a charitable response if you face up to your difficulties immediately.[19]

At the other extreme if you wait until the commencement of an adjourned proof you cannot expect the court to exercise its discretion in your favour.[20]

Common objections

1. Leading questions in examination-in-chief or re-examination

The question contains the answer not simply the topic to be answered. So wind-ups like:

> Q. Do you agree that ....?
> Q. Can I suggest to you that....................?

---

[19] *Cameron v. Lanarkshire Health Board* 1997 SLT 1040
[20] *Johnston v. Perth & Kinross Council* 2002 SCLR 558

Objections

>   Q.   Would it be fair to say that………………?

are sure signs that the questions will be leading. In fact use of any variant of the verb "to be" is also a giveaway.

>   Q.   Is it the case that…………………………?
>   Q.   Was it (dark)?

Be particularly alert for leading questions on re-examination.

2. No record

The general rule is that you don't require to plead evidence, but must give notice of the material facts on which you intend to rely. But you should not have to deal with trial by ambush. The test is whether on a generous view of the pleadings you should have anticipated the line of evidence and prepared for it, or are you being taken completely by surprise?

3. Questions relating to admissions on record

All admissions on record are sacrosanct, are agreed findings of fact and are off limits for examination. You must object to any line of questioning which might undermine the admission. In this regard note that "Believed to be true" is the equivalent of an admission.[21]

4. Questions relating to matters agreed in a joint minute

The same comments apply.

5. Compound questions

>   Q.   So you crossed the road and then walked into the jeweller's shop?

These are two distinct factual points. The witness should be asked these one at a time.

---

[21] *Binnie v Rederij Theodoro BV* 1993 SC 71.

Objections

6. Questions containing the personal opinion of the advocate

> Q. You told the court that you had an unrestricted view of the crossing. When I inspected the accident locus……………….

7. The question assumes facts not in evidence

Effectively the questioner misquotes what had been previously said by a witness.

8. The question relates to inadmissible evidence e.g. collateral facts

> Q. The allegation is that you drove without due care and attention on 1st January of last year. This is not the first time that this has happened is it?

9. The questioning and the line is unduly hostile, aggressive and personally insulting amounting to harassment of the witness

> Q. The truth is that you were having an affair with witness X, weren't you?

This might be a permissible question if you have material to that effect and the matter is relevant to motivation etc.

10. The question contains a comment on the evidence

When Sir Richard Muir commenced his cross-examination of the accused Fletcher he began as follows:

> "Now Mr Fletcher, we will have the truth."

This prompted the trenchant objection from Normal Birkett KC:

> "That is not a question, and it is charged with the most improper and unwarranted prejudice."[22]

---

[22] *The Oxford Book of Legal Anecdotes*, Oxford University Press, 1992.

Objections

11. Comments generally

It is quite easy to get into a habit of meeting each witness response with a comment such as "O.K", or "I understand" or "Thank you for that". The temptation is to use these as fillers. Technically these constitute comments on the witnesses' evidence and should be avoided.

12. Questions seeking opinion evidence from factual witnesses

Factual witnesses should not be asked about matters which require expertise. So a question like "What was the noise level in decibels?" is objectionable. However ordinary common sense impression evidence is not struck at. So the same witness might be asked whether it was noisy or not, or a factual witness might be asked:

> Q.   Did the driver seem drunk to you?

8 EXPERT WITNESSES

"How should the expert avoid becoming partisan in a process that makes no pretence of determining the truth but seeks only to weigh the persuasive effect of arguments deployed by one adversary or the other?
......the man who works the Three Card Trick is not cheating, nor does he incur any moral opprobrium, when he uses his sleight of hand to deceive the eye of the innocent rustic and to deny him the information he needs for a correct appraisal of what has gone on. The rustic does not have to join in; but if he chooses to, he is 'fair game'."

This was taken from an article which expert witness Mr Goodall was unwise enough to write some time before trial.

Mr Justice Laddie did not take kindly to his allotted role as country yokel.

"The whole basis of Mr Goodall's approach to the drafting of an expert's report is wrong. The function of a court of law is to discover the truth relating to the issues before it. In doing that it has to assess the evidence adduced by the parties. The judge is not a rustic who has chosen to play a game of Three Card Trick. He is not fair game. Nor is the truth." [23]

Planning the examination-in-chief

The essence of expert witness persuasion is the power of the witness to explain. The examination should be planned:

- To establish the authority of the expert as a person in whom the court can place its trust. This relates both to his qualifications and experience, and also to his independence and integrity.

---

[23] *Cala Homes (South) Limited and Others v Alfred McAlpine Homes East Limited* [1995] F.S.R. 818

- To have the expert testify as to the general background of his subject, hopefully referring to textbooks or other standard literature.

- To transition from the general to particular facts, usually with reference to a written report which has been lodged in process.

- To put to the expert any contrary opinion evidence for his comment.

An expert witness is allowed to give opinion evidence on matters outwith judicial knowledge. His qualifications for doing so can be scientific, vocational or simply practical. So by definition he will testify on matters outwith everyday experience. His role is not to usurp the judicial function, but to educate the judge on the topics and issues in dispute.

His most important qualifications should be:

1. Clarity of thought and expression.
2. The ability to explain his specialties in ways which enable the judge to make a reasoned decision.
3. Independence and integrity.

It is very easy for an expert to get sucked into the litigation process and to allow himself to identify with one side or another. Your first task in this area is to ensure that he knows his duty is to assist the court and not any party. He should understand and be guided by the so called "Ikarian Reefer"[24] principles, and in particular:

- Expert evidence should be the independent product of the expert uninfluenced by the exigencies of litigation.
- Experts should provide independent assistance to the court by way of unbiased opinion evidence.
- An expert witness should never assume the role of an advocate.

---

[24] *National Justice Compania Naviera SA v. Prudential Assurance Co. Ltd. (The Ikarian Reefer)* [1992] 2 Lloyd's Rep 68.

- Expert witnesses should state the facts upon which their opinion is based. They should not omit to consider material facts which might influence their concluded opinion.

- Experts must make it clear when a particular question falls outwith their expertise.

Dealing with your expert

In almost all cases your expert will have produced a report. You are not required to lodge this in advance, but generally it will be advantageous to do so. Familiarity with his own subject frequently leads the expert to make unwarranted assumptions about the levels of general knowledge. So wherever possible have the expert supplement the report with references to standard textbooks, Codes of Practice, British Standards and the like. Copy the extracts and lodge them. Prior to giving evidence you should either meet with the expert, or at least have had a detailed discussion with him about his evidence. He should have seen all the pleadings, all the statements, photographs and relevant information, and in particular all other expert reports.

Examination-in-chief

First of all qualify the witness as a person suitable to give opinion evidence. Obtain and lodge his CV before he starts his evidence. Then briefly lead him through it, asking if there are any particular matters which are relevant to the case in hand. In most cases there will be both professional and vocational qualifications. Where the expert has published any relevant material have him refer to it. Ask the expert directly if he knows what his duties are as an expert (having established in advance he does in fact know the correct answer!).

Before going to the report it is a useful preliminary to have the expert put matters in a general framework. If you want the court to take cognisance of any written material, for example, a scientific textbook, you will have to introduce the book through your expert.[25]

---

[25] *McTear v. Imperial Tobacco*, 2005 2 SC 1.

This means having him identify the publication and its provenance, and then putting the specific extract to him for his comment. That way the publication can be used to bolster and enhance the expert opinion. Otherwise you are not permitted in submissions to pluck passages from the publication as if they are evidence in the case. So in a case involving e.g. manual handling you might take him to the *Manual Handling Operations Regulations 1992* (as amended) - *Guidance on Regulations 2004* issued by the Health and Safety Executive, and have him testify on the general standards and expectations with regard to e.g. risk assessment, avoidance of manual handling and the like. After establishing the framework, tell the witness that you want to move from the general to the particular. Ask him to identify his "report no. 5/3 of process". Then take him through it. The report should list the sources of his information and instructions. Don't let him become too attached to any particular factual background. This is particularly important, because most expert reports proceed on a factual hypothesis which the expert has no way of knowing is true. He will almost certainly face cross-examination on different factual hypotheses. It is important that he deals with these fairly.

Typically an expert report will consist of numbered paragraphs. Ask the expert to read the paragraphs which you select. You may have reason not to want every paragraph to be put into the evidence. General matters may already have been dealt with in the preliminary introduction referred to above. Stop the witness at any point where you want him to explain matters. This might be at the end of a paragraph, but could equally be in the middle. Remember that the modern judge has a duty to engage with expert evidence, to understand it and if necessary to provide a reasoned acceptance or rebuttal of it. The whole thrust of your examination is to provide him with those reasons. These comment interludes, when you ask the expert to clarify and expand on his written report, provide the perfect opportunity for this ground work.

The ultimate question is for the court

You will already understand that the expert's role is to assist the court, not to replace it. The purpose of his evidence is to help the trier of fact to reach conclusions on factual matters by understanding the issues and the evidence. So it does not sit in the expert's mouth to say that conduct was negligent, or constituted malpractice, or was in breach of statutory duty. So don't frame any questions in these terms. But the reality is that such distinctions are paper thin and your judicious questioning on

Expert Witnesses

accepted standards, Codes of Practice or HSE Guidance should leave the sheriff with the smallest possible final step. It is quite permissible to ask a health and safety expert what statutes might be relevant to the issue, what in his opinion is a "dangerous" part of a machine or operation, and what an Approved Code of Practice says about the issue.

Cross-examination of experts

If cross-examination is the most difficult advocacy skill in cases at first instance, cross-examination of experts is the most difficult aspect of cross-examination.

Aims of cross-examination of experts

You will very rarely have any prospect of knocking down an expert witness. Your ambitions should be much more modest. As a general rule you will be asking the court in submissions to *prefer* your expert. You will do this by means of a tightly controlled cross-examination concentrating on areas where you have material with which to control and confront the witness. You must have a plan and you must stick to it. Your cross should be limited to a small area where you can hold your own using leading questions. Don't be tempted to leave this enclave. You are dealing with a person whose knowledge and experience of the subject far outweigh your own, and who will leave you floundering if you try to engage with him on matters at large. So use leading questions wherever possible.

As a general rule never ask an expert witness a "Why" question in cross. Once you start to examine the expert using open questions you give him complete leeway to attack and devastate your position.

Cross-examination as to independence or bias

Frequency of instruction and payment, professional pride in one's own handiwork, or simple *amour propre* when one's opinion is being doubted make it almost inevitable that many experts fail to reach the Olympian heights of independence required of them in the Ikarian Reefer principles. It is one thing to suspect this, and quite another to show it. In this jurisdiction there is very little mileage to be gained in an outright attack on integrity or independence. It is perfectly proper that experts are paid and in *McTear* v. *Imperial Tobacco*[26] an allegation that the defenders' experts were the paid mouthpieces of the tobacco industry spectacularly misfired. Not only did the court expect that experts should be compensated, the fact that the pursuer's experts were unpaid left them open to a charge of zealotry. You may think that the well established conduits between the insurance industry and certain medical experts might be a fruitful ground for cross-examination, but the overwhelming likelihood is that any questioning will be met by a bland assurance that the expert acts for both pursuer and defenders. The effect on the court is that you have made an unsavoury allegation which you cannot bring home. So unless you have smoking gun material on bias, you should leave this alone.

Preparing the cross-examination

Find out everything the opposing expert has ever said or written on the subject in hand. Start off with a Google search against his name, and then move onto Google Scholar. Obtain the relevant articles. Check against the scotcourts website for previous testimony by the expert. You might well find out, for example, that a particular medical witness does not believe that a condition like Carpal Tunnel Syndrome can ever be work related, contrary to current medical thinking, or that the expert's particular area of specialism relates to paediatric, and not orthopaedic trauma. You cannot use material from a previous case to show that his or her expert opinion was not accepted in the past. You can use it to know the likely parameters of his evidence, and to set your own boundaries by using his prior publications or testimony to prevent any radical differences of approach in your own case.

Topics and order for cross-examination

- **Seek concessions**
  As always you will require to do this at the commencement of the cross-examination. Have the opposing expert confirm that your own expert is suitably qualified to provide opinion evidence on the topic. Most experts will agree that there might be a range of possible views on any particular subject. The most important area of concession seeking relates to established standards, procedures or orthodoxies.

---

[26] 2005 S.C.1

- **Fix the normative boundaries**

    So you might have the expert agree that the standards for assessing the work of an orthopaedic surgeon are contained in the British Orthopaedic Association "Blue Book", that the vigilance expected of a heavy goods driver is contained in the DSA Guide[27] and that the agreed procedure for assessing noise induced hearing loss is contained in the Kings, Cole & Lutman medico-legal guidelines book.[28] You don't need to have the expert agree that the contents of a textbook are correct. What you are doing is establishing the sound, broadly based consensus of the scientific community. If the expert wants to argue that the consensus is wrong you can impeach him as a maverick. Galileo was proved right in the end, but unless the maverick expert is of a similar pre-eminence in his field, it is unlikely that he will carry the day in court against the current accepted orthodoxy.

- **Use of supporting literature**

    Occasionally this kind of expert will seek to bolster up his evidence by reference to articles which have not been lodged. This is objectionable for a number of reasons. As a matter of notice every publication on which he is relying should have been lodged in advance.[29] Secondly as noted above, unless a passage from the textbook is specifically adopted by the witness, it does not become part of the evidence. Finally be alert not to allow the court to become a forum for what is simply the promulgation of a theory. See for instance, the case of *Sienkiewicz v. Greif (UK) Ltd* [2011] 2 A.C. 229 at 299:

    > "What the testimony (on the causes of mesothelioma) amounted to was the promotion of a theory rather than the establishment of facts and it did not constitute evidence on which reliable conclusions could be made."

---

[27] *Driving Standards Agency, 9th Edition, 2009.*

[28] *Assessment of Hearing Disability; Guidelines for medicolegal practice,* Whurr publishers, 1992

[29] *Main v. McAndrew Wormald Ltd* 1988 SLT 141.

Henry Kissinger once observed that:

> "The reason academic politics are so bitter is that so little is at stake."

Many medical controversies fall into the same category, with researchers publishing and adopting contrary theoretical positions which never truly impinge on diagnosis or practical medicine. It is only in the rarest of cases that you will become involved in trying to resolve any genuine academic or medical controversy.

It is accepted that medical experts may refer to publications in a separate but related field to bolster their opinion.[30]

You can then read extracts from the publication and ask the witness for his comments. He may wish to take issue with what is said. Don't let yourself become engaged in a scientific controversy. Simply insist that he answers the question whether or not the publication represents the current scientific consensus.

- **Expert qualifications**

Check what the opposing experts' qualifications mean and that they are relevant. Frequently experts' CVs are full of all kinds of sales puffery, which are not at all relevant to the issue. Membership of the Institute of Directors seems to be a particular favourite. Have your own expert identify what the initials mean. This may give you a platform to suggest, for example, that a generalist health and safety advisor would defer in practice to an acoustics specialist. Remember that you are seeking to have the court *prefer* your expert, bearing in mind that reasons will have to be given. True eminence in experience, qualifications or simply job title, e.g. professor, might well provide the route.

---

[30] *ibid.*

- **Check the factual assumptions**

    Most expert evidence proceeds on a hypothesis. If facts A or B are established, then his or her view is that C will follow. The best attack on the expert's opinion may be to undermine the facts on which it is based. So the examination would proceed along these lines:

    Q. You were supplied with sales figures which contained an estimate for the next year's projected profits for the card shop, weren't you?
    Q. That estimate was prepared on the basis that business conditions would remain unchanged, wasn't it?
    Q. You prepared your report on that basis, didn't you?
    Q. You weren't aware that shortly after the estimate was prepared, a cut price "Cards 2 Go" shop was about to open less than 50 yards away?
    Q. That would have a significant effect on the future turnover, wouldn't it?
    Q. That would have a significant effect on future profits?

If the expert wants to quibble that this wouldn't have changed his view you can follow up by saying:

    Q. There really isn't any information regarding business conditions which would change your mind, is there?

- **Does the expert know the nature of his role?**

    Most expert reports now come with a standard boilerplate of declarations that the expert knows his duties to the court etc. So there will generally be little mileage in directly suggesting that he views his role as that of hired gun. But there are other signs which advertise that the author of the report does not properly understand his function. Reports which conclude that the defender was at fault, or in breach of statutory duty, or which seek to apportion negligence are a godsend to the cross examiner. They show that the expert doesn't really understand that these are matters solely for the court.

Similarly from time to time you might see reports which contain extracts from precognitions together with a running commentary on the statements. Road traffic reports seem particularly prone to this solecism. It is not the expert's job to assess the truth of factual statements and in making any such comment the expert is not exercising any particular expertise.[31] Object to any attempt to turn the proceedings from trial by judge to trial by expert.

---

[31] See e.g. the case of *Liddell v. Middleton* [1996] PIQR P36

9 THE HEARING ON EVIDENCE

"Facts are stubborn things; and whatever may be our wishes, our inclinations and the dictates of our passion, they cannot alter the state of the facts and evidence."

John Adams in *Argument in Defense of the Soldiers in the Boston Massacre Trials*, December, 1770.

Adams was later the second President of the United States.

The hearing on evidence gives you the opportunity to pull together all the disparate strands of evidence in the case, to marshal these in their most persuasive format, and to present a compelling argument to the court. In most cases you will know before the proof commences the factual framework you must prove to meet the legal requirements. The task now is to extract, order and present the evidence in the strongest possible light to support that framework.

You will have already prepared your outline submissions founded mainly on your expectations of how your own evidence would emerge. You will now have to adapt this to the actual testimony before the court, including the evidence from the other side. Your argument should be structured and you should announce this structure to the court. If at all possible prepare final written submissions and present these to the court on the morning. These submissions are not a formal step in process, and you shouldn't worry about any infelicity of presentation. The court will be grateful for any kind of written material at this stage. A suggested format for the submissions might be as follows:

1. Outstanding objections to evidence heard under reservation.
2. Outline draft findings in fact.
3. Detailed comments on the evidence.
4. Legal authorities on the substantive issues.
5. A schedule of damages together with supporting case references.

The Hearing on Evidence

1. **Outstanding objections**

If evidence has been heard under reservation, the court will expect you to make your submissions as to whether it should be admitted. Suppose there has been evidence which you consider inadmissible because it is collateral to the issue in hand. The current test is whether such evidence is probative of any of the issues at proof with the leading Scottish case being *Strathmore Group v. Credit Lyonnais*.[32] Prepare a lever arch binder with each case separated by a divider. Make up a frontispiece showing the names of cases in a numbered list. So in the above example the first case might be *Strathmore Group v. Credit Lyonnais* under a topic heading of "Evidence under Reservation". Further cases might be listed under a separate topic heading, for example, "Substantive law on the Management of Health and Safety at Work Regulations 1999".

2. **Outline findings in fact**

Unlike the court of session, a sheriff is obliged by OCR 12.2(3) to prepare findings in fact. These are the central building blocks on which your legal case must be constructed. The strong recommendation is that you prepare a written outline of proposed findings in fact. You don't need to bother about the formal aspects of the judgement, such as the description of the parties, but you should direct the content to the central areas of dispute. Wherever possible set these out with the source of the evidence identified, for example:

i. On 18th June the pursuer attended Monklands Hospital at 6.40 a.m. and was seen in Accident & Emergency Triage at 6.47 a.m. (evidence of the pursuer; records of Monklands Hospital, pursuer's Inventory 5/2 at page 95).

ii. She remained there as an inpatient in the Orthopaedic Ward until 25th June. (records of Monklands Hospital, pursuer's Inventory 5/2 at pp 97-105.)

---

[32] 1994 SLT 1023

In complex cases consider investing in a software programme like CaseMap which will prepare factual timelines with reference to evidential source material.

3. Comments on the evidence

One method is to deal with the evidence of each witness *seriatim*, with commendation or criticism, and exhortations to the sheriff to accept or reject. This method is better than nothing, but that is all. The problem is that it is very difficult to use this format to promote and sustain any kind of argument.

A better approach is to make up the Core Factual Matrix as it has emerged in the evidence, and then seek to assess the critical areas of dispute in the light of the undisputed or indisputable evidence. So there will be areas of the case where there is broad agreement on the facts, or where documentary or other evidence means that they cannot realistically be in contention. Ask the court to assess the remaining evidence insofar as it fits with the Core Factual Matrix. This means organising the submission by factual topic, for example:

Did an accident occur at all?

> "Although there are no witnesses to the accident, the pursuer attended at Monklands Hospital at 6.40 a.m. the following day when she complained of acute back strain. On examination in Triage she was found to have objective evidence of lumbar tenderness."

Then deal with the evidence of the percipient witnesses on the point, emphasising in particular independence or bias, opportunity for observation, and what the witness has said on previous occasions. Does the evidence of this witness fit with the rest of the evidence? Some sheriffs think that credibility and reliability are matters solely for them. It is not your job to tell the court that the witness seemed shifty. But you are entitled to and should address issues of credibility. Witnesses do not have to be accepted on every aspect of their testimony, for instance, where a particularly dramatic fall was spoken to by an eyewitness, his passage of evidence in this regard was accepted, although he was confused on other aspects. The highly dramatic fall was something which he would have remembered.[33]

---

[33] *Pate's Curator ad Litem v. Stewart Homes (Scotland) Ltd* [2013] CSOH 30.

The Hearing on Evidence

A frequent distinction is that witnesses who are credible, that is, doing their best to tell the truth, may not be reliable. Finally you must deal with the expert evidence in the case. Did the expert meet the Ikarian Reefer standards, especially with regard to independence and integrity? Was he apprised of all the relevant facts? Does your expert's practical experience or his pre-eminence in the field mean that he should be preferred?

4. The legal authorities

These should be in a lever arch binder separated by dividers. Where possible use a highlighting tool to emphasise particular passages on which you wish to found. As indicated in Chapter 2 there are some authorities to which you must make reference, otherwise it is a matter of judgement. Usually you will also want to provide a general textbook extract which covers the broad area of law, before delving into the detailed case reports.

5. Schedule of damages

In a personal injury case this should be in the prescribed form P16 for ordinary actions, or 10e for summary causes. You are not limited to what you previously put down in your statement of valuation. You should have an interest calculation on damages from the accident date to the date of proof. The usual method is for interest to run at 4% on past solatium where the injury is ongoing, and thereafter at 8% from the date of recovery. Where the ongoing injuries are sustained in a single accident most of the solatium (e.g. two thirds) will be allocated to the past, so interest runs only on that amount. The first port of call for *solatium* is now the Judicial College (current edition is the 12th edition) formerly the Judicial Studies Board or JSB Guidelines supplemented by particular cases. In other cases e.g. breach of contract where damages are not for a specific crystallised sum, provide a worked schedule showing the basis of your calculations.

10 INCIDENTAL AND PROCEDURE ROLL ADVOCACY

"If it takes a lot of words to say what you had in mind, give it more thought."
Dennis Roth

"Be sincere, be brief, be seated."
Franklin D. Roosevelt

Much of your sheriff court work will involve moving and opposing motions, incidental applications, and other miscellaneous hearing such as legal debates. These require a different set of persuasive skills from the cut and thrust of examination and cross-examination of witnesses. Some of the same general rules apply.

1. Look at the person you are trying to persuade, in this case the sheriff. This does not mean a locked gaze, but make direct eye contact from time to time and keep your head up and out of your papers.
2. By all means have a prepared written outline and occasionally a written skeleton argument which you will put up to the court, but never have a script, and don't read your submission.
3. Get quickly to the point. Sheriff courts are extremely busy places of work. Don't waste anyone's time. Be organised, be brief, and say it only once.

A motion may be contested by an opponent, who will be present in court, or you may be seeking an order on which the sheriff wishes to be addressed.

In the former case you are likely to find yourself in a court room full of other agents with a lengthy court roll containing a variety of cases. If you are far down the list, don't disappear for coffee, but rather stay and observe how the sheriff disposes of the other cases before your own. See how some agents appear effortlessly to have

Incidental and Procedure Roll Advocacy

the ear of the court. Watch, listen and learn. Sheriff courts everywhere are under stringent time constraints with a volume of disposals to be made each day. The need for brevity and expedition is paramount. You are in a place of business, not a debating chamber.

1. Introduce yourself, frame the issue and tell the court what you want

Although "May it please the court" is a time honoured introduction recognised throughout the common law world, it is archaic to modern ears, and is rarely used in the sheriff court. Instead simply say:

> "Good morning my lord, Marshall for the pursuer, and my friend Ms McEachan appears for the defenders."

In many courts there is a preliminary call-over of all cases in the hope that matters have been resolved by agents without the need for further argument. This leaves the truly contentious matters held over to be heard later that day. If you have seen that this is the practice ask the sheriff if he wishes your case to be held over with the other contested business. Only after you have been given permission to proceed, should you commence your substantive argument. As concisely as possible, indicate to the court what the case is about, give a brief procedural history and specify the nature of the order you are seeking today.

2. Prepare an outline written submission

In any matter which is remotely complicated you should prepare an outline written argument and tender it to the court with a copy for your opponent. This is emphatically not a word for word script. You cannot read and think at the same time, and you will be unable to make any kind of eye contact with your head buried in a transcript. Rather it is a document drafted in headline or bullet point format which takes the court quickly to the nub of the argument.

3. Copy and highlight legal authorities

The first port of call on any procedural matter will be *Macphail's Sheriff Court Practice* (3rd Edition) which enjoys a biblical status amongst bar and bench. Whilst the sheriff is likely to have it before him, spare him the trouble of opening it by putting up the relevant copy extract. If there are other authorities on which you wish to rely, have them copied and put everything in a small lever arch folder, with separators. Highlight the important passages using a standard yellow highlighter. Your objective is to lead the sheriff as quickly as possible to your main points, and to make the decision as easy as possible.

4. Don't save anything for rebuttal

Start and stick to your strongest argument. There was an obituary about a famous judge of whom it was said that advocates didn't need to labour a point before him on six or seven separate occasions; three or four times was enough. Don't believe it. Say it once and as strongly as possible right from the start.

5. Listen closely and politely to your opponent's submission

You will generally be given a right of rebuttal. Try to deal with any new points which have been made. Frequently at this stage the sheriff will give you an idea as to his thinking and address any points which appear to cause concern. If you are asked a question, you must answer it as best you can. Otherwise keep it brief and sit down.

The sheriff will then dispose of the matter. If you have been successful you should be entitled to the expenses of the motion on the basis that it is the opposition to your motion which has required the case to call. The court will not award expenses unless you ask for them. Seek the expenses of the contested motion.

The Procedure Roll Hearing

In general litigation a debate on the procedure roll will only be allowed after an options hearing (OCR 9.12(3)(c). The party moving for a debate will have to satisfy the court that there is a realistic prospect of dismissal of the cause, or of the defences (the so-called "knock-out blow"), or alternatively a realistic opportunity to delete significant averments which would result in a saving of time, expense and inconvenience to witnesses.[34] In personal injury litigation a defender wishing to take a case to debate should lodge a notice of opposition to the motion for proof (OCR 36.G1(7)). The notice should detail the reasons for the opposition. Minor

---

[34] *Gracey v. Sykes* 1994 SCLR 909

points of specification should not be enough to take the case to debate. At the diet of debate your opponent cannot raise new matters except on cause shown (OCR 22.1(4)) and should be restricted to the issues raised in the note of basis of preliminary plea, or his notice of opposition to the motion for proof.

Preparation for debate

There will almost certainly be a Practice Note in your jurisdiction obliging you to lodge a list of authorities prior to the debate. You will not be taken by surprise at a legal debate, but what you must prepare for is questioning, probing and interrogation by the sheriff. You must expect your propositions, case theories and legal submissions to be put under rigorous scrutiny. It is sometimes difficult to see the problems with your arguments from your side of the board. Wherever possible prepare by discussion of the issues with a legal colleague.

Relevancy and specification at debate

The debate proceeds on the basis that your averments are true, and your opponent must argue that your case will necessarily fail notwithstanding.[35] The court will look at your averments, matters which are admitted in your opponents' pleadings, or matters believed to be true which are taken as the equivalent of admissions.[36]

Otherwise it is not permissible to rely on your opponent's pleadings in argument to the court. Further at this stage you are entitled to ask the court to draw only the most favourable inferences from the facts, even although there may be other inferences available from the facts after proof.[37] In personal injury actions dismissal of a case on relevancy is extremely rare, and the court will be reluctant to say there is no common law negligence without hearing the facts. This kind of legal hearing is a stringent intellectual exercise, but the same general principles of organisation apply. You should make up a List of Authorities sorted by topic heading for example:

---

[35] *Jamieson v Jamieson* 1952 S.C. (HL) 44
[36] *Binnie v. Rederij Theodoro BV* 1993 S.C. 71.
[37] *Wilson v. Norwich Union Fire Insurance Society Limited* (No. 1) 1999 SLT 1139.

Incidental and Procedure Roll Advocacy

1. General relevancy at Debate
    1.1 *Jamieson v. Jamieson*

2. The Occupiers' Liability (Scotland) Act 1960
    2.1 *Gallagher v. Kleinwort Benson (Trustees) Ltd* 2003 SCLR 384.

etc.

The skeleton argument – looks matter!

You should prepare an outline skeleton argument but not a word for word submission. It should be organised by topics. The topic description should be underlined. Thereafter the argument should be a precise summary of the submissions to be developed, and should have a numbered list of the points which you wish to make. The hearing will almost certainly develop into a dialogue between you and the sheriff. Reading from a script will shut down the thinking part of your brain which has to provide the responses to the questioning which will inevitably ensue. The authorities for the court should be put in a lever arch folder, with separators for each case. Highlight the particular passages on which you are relying with a yellow highlighter. You will want to skim through the familiar general authorities e.g. *Jamieson*, and concentrate on the cases particular and pertinent to the cause. As you introduce each of those cases, read the rubric, sum up briefly the essentials of the case, then turn to the particular passages on which you rely. The temptation is to read far too quickly. It can be unnerving at first to listen to your own voice reading out long passages from cases. Your eye tends to get ahead of your voice causing you to speed up. This is a mistake. Keep a steady pace. At the end of each case sum up its relevance to your particular argument e.g. "So the pursuer takes from *Lynx Express Parcels* that liability for failed equipment is strict……………………."

Conduct of the debate

The party who is criticising the averments will go first. None of the arguments should come as a surprise to you. You will find that most sheriffs will interrupt your opponent's submissions with questions which go to the heart of the matter. By the time you rise to speak, she may have already formed a preliminary view, and be clear of the areas where assistance is required. This will frequently mean that you will perforce be taken out of the prepared order of your skeleton argument. Do not

Incidental and Procedure Roll Advocacy

under any circumstances cavil at this, and insist on proceeding in the order of your script. No one is interested. If your skeleton argument is prepared on a topic basis, you should be able to go straight to the points you are asked about. Frequently you will be asked a hypothetical question, generally seeking to extrapolate and examine the limits of your proposition. If you are asked a question you must deal with it there and then.

In *Kennedy v. Norwich Union Fire Insurance Society Ltd* [38] it was stated:

> "…………………..a judge does not have to sit sphinx–like, silent and inscrutable, giving no indication of how his mind is working or what impact the submissions are making upon him. It is perfectly proper, during the debate, for a judge to give 'clear indications' on the apparent strength and persuasiveness of the arguments advanced on all sides."

In the course of the debate most sheriffs will give an indication of the way in which their minds are working, and at the very least what matters are troubling them. You may be able to address any concerns there and then with a simple minute of amendment, and if it is brief there is no reason why you should not amend orally. For more substantial matters you will need to seek leave to amend and to present later a formal minute of amendment. In that event you should suggest to the sheriff that instead of fixing a fresh debate, he should simply continue the present debate hearing for further procedure, including possible amendment. This was the approved course in *Kennedy*. If he agrees then the matter will at least call again before someone who is familiar with the arguments.

If you can't tell which way the wind is blowing, you must await the written judgement. If your case is dismissed, or critical averments excluded, you should consider an appeal, frequently accompanied by a minute of amendment addressing any pleadings deficiencies.

---

[38] 1993 S.C. 578 at p585

11 APPELLATE ADVOCACY

"What, then do we notice about judges' opinions? Sometimes, of course, a particular passage stands out and is frequently cited simply because it contains a useful summary of the case law on a particular topic. In the Inner House of the Court of Session, for instance, all the copies of 1947 Session Cases fall open at the page of report of Thomas v. Thomas where Lord Thankerton summarises the approach which an appeal court should take when asked to review a first instance judge's finding in fact."

Lord Rodger: *The Form and Language of Judicial Opinions*,
Law Quarterly Review 2002 at page 242.

Appellate advocacy is the most difficult exercise in persuasion you will ever undertake. It requires a different mind-set from that deployed in the examination of witnesses and even procedure roll advocacy. There is already a decision before the court, which you will be asking the appeal court either to uphold or reverse. Most appeals fail. Frequently the reason is not that the appeal court necessarily agrees with the judge at first instance but because they decline to interfere. So before any steps are taken you must familiarise with the boundaries of interference (and where there might be gaps in the fences).

The boundaries of appellate advocacy

An appeal is not a re-hearing. Generally the question will not be whether the sheriff was correct to reach his decision but whether he was *entitled* to do so. Where you have to appeal that the facts have been wrongly found, you must be prepared to argue that the original decision was "plainly wrong". If you are acting for a respondent, then the adjudication privileges which attach to a judge at first instance should be constantly kept before the court.

Appellate Advocacy

Successful appellate advocacy depends on having a clear idea of the principles on which an appellate court can act.

The following is a very brief outline of typical areas.

1. Appeals on interlocutory decisions

In this event you will generally be asking the court to overturn an exercise of discretion. This means that you will have to persuade the court that the sheriff has been influenced by some extraneous matter, has failed to take into account some relevant matter or is otherwise plainly wrong. Generally the weight to be attached to each issue is a matter for the court at first instance.

2. Appeals on findings of fact

The traditional formulation for overturning findings in fact is contained in *Thomas v. Thomas*[39]. This is the well-thumbed page referred to by Lord Rodger in the quotation at the start of this chapter.

> "(1) Where a question of fact has been tried by a Judge without a jury, and there is no question of misdirection of himself by the Judge, an appellate Court which is disposed to come to a different conclusion on the printed evidence should not do so unless it is satisfied that any advantage enjoyed by the trial Judge by reason of having seen and heard the witnesses could not be sufficient to explain or justify the trial Judge's conclusion.
> (2) The appellate Court may take the view that, without having seen or heard the witnesses, it is not in a position to come to any satisfactory conclusion on the printed evidence.
> (3) The appellate Court, either because the reasons given by the trial Judge are not satisfactory, or because it unmistakably so appears from the evidence, may be satisfied that he has not taken proper advantage of having seen and heard the witnesses, and the matter will then become at large for the appellate court. It is obvious that the value and importance of having seen and heard the witnesses will vary according to the class of case, and, it may be, the individual case in question."

---

[39] 1947 S.C. (H.L.) at page 54

Appellate Advocacy

The appeal court will expect you to know this passage. Unless you can fit your appeal points into this framework you have no realistic prospects. There is also a distinction to be made between primary findings in fact (e.g. what a witness observed) and inferential findings in fact (e.g. what was reasonably foreseeable in the circumstances). You will have a much better chance of overturning the latter. See the case of *Brodie v. British Railways Board*[40] for a useful checklist.

3. Appeals on errors in law

You will be arguing that the sheriff has misdirected himself on some matter of law. So the Inner House overturned a sheriff who failed to treat a static barrier as work equipment which was "in use", in terms of the Provision and Use of Work Equipment Regulations 1998,[41] where a judge at first instance had wrongly applied an economic test as to whether work equipment was suitable[42] or where a sheriff following debate had made specific factual inferences on the reasonable conduct of insurers, instead of hearing evidence on the matter.[43]

4. Quantum of damages

You will have to show that there has been some error in principle, for instance, that calculation of interest has been approached on the wrong basis. With regard to solatium, the appeal court will interfere only where the award is disproportionate or outwith the range of reasonable awards.

5. Contributory negligence

You will have to show that there has been error in principle of the approach taken to contributory negligence and that a substantial alteration to the percentage figures is required to do justice to the parties. So in a case where a child was knocked down the Inner House was not prepared to change the apportionment for contributory negligence from 20%. A motor car is always more dangerous to others than a

---

[40] 1972 SLT Notes 37.
[41] *Johnston v. Amec Construction Ltd* 2010 Rep LR 96.
[42] *Skinner v. The Scottish Ambulance Service*, 2004 SC 790.
[43] *Wilson v. Norwich Union* 199 SLT 1139.

pedestrian, and there was no error in principle in the judge's approach.[44]

6. Expenses

Appeals on expenses are particularly discouraged.[45] Generally you will have to identify some error of principle, for example, where the judge at first instance has failed to consider the effect of interest when calculating whether a tender had been defeated or not.[46]

Appeals in summary causes

A special word of warning relates to these appeals. The procedure is contained in S.C.R. 25. The most important point to remember is that an appeal from a final judgement is available on a point of law only.[47] This severely restricts any opportunity for appellate interference. The sheriff's findings of fact are generally inviolate, unless they can be approached as a point of law. So in a negligence action you might reasonably argue that the sheriff has wrongly admitted a line of evidence leading to findings (a), (b) and (c), which might put the issue at large before the appeal court as a matter of law. But you cannot otherwise argue that the sheriff was wrong to find (a) or (b) or (c) from properly admitted evidence, because that is purely a question of fact.

The grounds of appeal

In terms of OCR 31.4.1, any note of appeal in a sheriff court ordinary cause must be in Form A1. It must contain the full grounds of appeal and may be amended without leave up until 14 days before the appeal. The grounds should be set out as numbered paragraphs and should be comprehensive. You will almost certainly not be allowed to develop any new grounds on the day. The grounds of appeal should not themselves contain argument or case references, but should be numbered propositions. Where possible start with the major premise (general proposition of

---

[44] *McCluskey v. Wallace* 1998 SLT 711
[45] *Caldwell v. Dykes* 1906 8F 839
[46] *Manson v. Skinner* 2002 SLT 448
[47] *Sheriff Courts (Scotland) Act* 1971 S31A

law) before moving to the minor premise which applies to your case. So, for example:

> "1. Regulation 4 of the Personal Protective Equipment at Work Regulations 1992 requires that an employer should provide personal protective equipment where there is a risk of injury which is not adequately controlled" (*major premise*). Any adequate risk assessment would have shown that the operations carried out by the pursuer at the material time carried a risk of injury. Full length gauntlets should have been provided in terms of the Personal Protective Equipment at Work Regulations 1992. (*minor premise*).

Preparation for Appeal – The Note of Argument

Should your appeal argument be purely oral or written?

There is no requirement in the sheriff court to lodge any note of argument, unlike appeals before the Inner House. There are a number of reasons why you should provide one. It forces you to consider the structure of your appeal and to put matters in a coherent order as opposed to simply a succession of points. It allows you to frame the issues in the format you hope the court will adopt. It is a permanent document which summarises your position, which the court will see before the appeal commences, and will take away before writing the judgement. So it is always worthwhile to take some time over its composition. Avoid all rhetorical flourishes. Don't use the first draft. Let it marinade a bit before finalising the document.

As to presentation you should follow the principles set out in the Inner House Practice Note (September 2011) at paragraph 86:

1. A note of argument should be a concise summary of the submissions to be developed.
2. It should contain a numbered list of the points which the party wishes to make.
3. Each point should be followed by a reference to any transcript of evidence or other document on which the party wishes to rely. The note of argument should identify the relevant passage in the document in question.

Appellate Advocacy

4. A note of argument should state, in respect of each authority cited:
   (a) the proposition of law that the authority demonstrates; and
   (b) the parts of the authority (identified by page or paragraph references) that support the proposition.
5. More than one authority should not be cited in support of a given proposition unless the additional citation is necessary for a proper presentation of the argument.

Preparation for Appeal – Miscellaneous

The exact time for lodging any note of authorities varies in terms of the Practice Notes for various sheriffdoms, all of which are contained in the Parliament House Book. You will require to lodge your list of authorities prior to the appeal hearing and you should send a copy to the other side. There is no requirement in the sheriff court for the bundle of authorities to be lodged prior to the hearing, but again it makes good advocacy sense to lodge a lever arch folder with all the authorities to which you wish to refer separated out and the relevant passages highlighted. In an appeal from the facts you will require to lodge a transcript of the shorthand notes. You must be prepared to argue the appeal with reference to specific passages from the notes. Separately, there may be a number of productions to which you wish to refer. Whilst these will be part of the court process it will save a lot of trouble if you extract the particular productions to which you intend to refer and to make up a separate appendix of those specific productions, with a copy for the court and for your opponent.

The Advocacy Presentation in Court

The Inner House Practice Note refers to submissions which "are to be developed". The note of argument will be the starting point for your oral advocacy before the court. You will flesh out the argument with examples, hypotheses and case law during your presentation. The organisation of the note should be topic based. There is no hiding place in appellate advocacy. You will have to prepare to be interrogated on every aspect of the argument. If you are asked a question, you must do your best to answer it there and then. Do not under any circumstances tell the court that you will come to that matter in due course. Where the evidence has been brief the sheriff principal might have read the full shorthand transcript, but you should act on the presumption that she hasn't. You should have already referred to the specific passages, for example: 96A-E in the note of argument, but the appeal will not be limited to the passages to which you want to refer. Typically you will be asked a question such as:

> Q. Where does the expert say that an early inspection was indicated?

You must be able to answer this, not in a general sense such as "Earlier in the cross-examination", but with reference to a specific passage. So in complicated cases where the facts are under discussion you should always make your own précis of the witness evidence with specific page references for important points. This means that when the appeal develops into a dialogue, you can instantly refer to the appropriate passage. Finally be clear about what you want. If you are seeking to amend, delete or amplify findings in fact you should prepare a separate written note specifying the findings sought.

Presentation in court

A suitable structure for your advocacy presentation where you have already lodged a note of argument might be as follows:-

- Outline to the court a brief procedural history.
- Indicate what you will be asking the court to do at the end of your submissions.
- Where you are seeking to amend, delete or amplify findings in fact present a note of the proposed findings at the commencement.[48]
- Refer to the note of argument. Amplify the note with reference to specific evidential passages identified by page and paragraph number from the transcript.
- Indicate the section in the sheriff's judgement which deals with those passages and be prepared to argue that he is wrong.
- Identify to the court the passage or passages where the sheriff has given reasons for his decision, and argue that these are misconceived.
- Argue that having regard to these errors, the issue is now at large for the appellate court.

---

[48] *Marshall v. William Sharp and Sons Ltd.,* 1991 SLT 114.

- If the matter is now at large for the court, specify the order sought.
- Where you are seeking to delete, supplement or add to the findings in fact have a pre-printed note with your specific suggestions.
- Seek the expenses of the appeal.

Rebuttal

If you have gone first, you may be given a right of reply after your opponent's submissions. You should always wait until you are invited by the court to reply. If you do reply, resist the temptation to go over the same ground as covered in your original submission, and address only those areas where you think your opponent might have made some traction. Be brief. Sit down.

12 FAMILY AND DOMESTIC RELATIONS ADVOCACY

by Claire Anne McFadden*, principal solicitor at
J.K.Cameron Solicitors, Glasgow.

"The Family Division teemed with strange differences, special pleading, intimate half-truths, exotic accusations,………. fine grained particularities of circumstance needed to be assimilated at speed. Parents… were dazed to find themselves in vicious combat with the one they once loved. And waiting offstage, boys and girls… huddling together while the gods above them fought to the last…"

Ian McEwan, *The Children Act*
Jonathan Cape, London 2014.

The purpose of this chapter is to provide a brief overview of the kind of situations in family litigation where your advocacy skills might be deployed, and how best you might approach those hearings. Good advocacy requires good preparation. Matters of substantive law are dealt with only in passing. All of the advice provided in the preceding chapters regarding advocacy in civil cases applies in family actions.

Family law and domestic relations litigation involve a wide range of court proceedings many of which are different from the conventional civil action. You will find in practice that most of the cases requiring your advocacy skills will relate to children. Whilst actions concerning divorce, cohabitation or dissolution of civil partnerships are common in the sheriff court, many of these cases are undefended. Where they are defended, advocacy is often limited to routine procedural callings leading up to proof and then conduct of the proof itself. More frequently, you will be involved in advocacy at different stages of actions involving children which is what the bulk of this chapter will address. The same principles of advocacy in child actions can be applied to divorce, cohabitation, and protective orders cases. The legislative framework in these other types of cases will be different but the overall objectives of the court rules and Practice Notes will be very similar.

1. General Principles in Cases Involving Children

The overarching principles applying in child cases are well established by legislation[49] and are clearly enunciated in case law. When coming to a decision about a matter relating to a child, the court (or Children's Hearing) must:

1. have regard to the need to safeguard and promote the welfare of the child throughout childhood as the paramount consideration (in adoption matters the consideration is 'throughout the child's lifetime');
2. so far as practicable, taking account of the child's age and maturity, give the child an opportunity to express his views and have regard to those views,
3. not make any order unless it considers that it would be better for the child that the order be made, and
4. make expeditious progress in the cause.[50]

The court is also required to have regard to the need to protect the child from abuse or the risk of abuse, to consider the likelihood of abuse, its effect upon the child, the ability of a perpetrator to meet the needs of the child and the effect of any abuse (or risk of it) upon a person caring for or having contact with the child.[51] Furthermore, regard must be had to the provisions of the European Convention on Human Rights.[52]

---

[49] See section 11(7) of the Children (Scotland) Act 1995. These are echoed at sections 25 and 27-29 of the Children's Hearing (Scotland) Act 2011, and also in sections 14, 28 and 84 of the Adoption and Children (Scotland) Act 2007.
[50] Section 11(7) of the Children (Scotland) Act 1995
[51] Section 11(7B) of the Children (Scotland) Act 1995 as amended by the Family Law (Scotland) Act 2006
[52] Since the Human Rights Act 1998 incorporated the Convention into domestic law, making its provisions directly enforceable, issues may arise in family cases regarding the courts compliance with the Convention and the decisions of the European Court. Article 6 affords protections to individuals (including children) involved in litigation in respect of fairness and appropriateness. Article 8 deals explicitly with family life and the safeguards concerning the state's interference with an individual's right to respect for private family life.

Family and Domestic Relations Advocacy

Procedural Framework

A comprehensive framework for expeditious progress of cases has been formed through revised court rules, Practice Notes and decisions from the Inner House and Supreme Court.[53] The framework is intended to keep agents and parties firmly focussed on the earliest possible resolution of a child's case. This responsibility rests, in the main, with the parties and their agents. Sheriffs require to ensure that agents and parties conduct cases with due regard to economy and restraint.

The emphasis on timescales and economic use of resources places considerable time pressures upon agents. It is critical that you appreciate the 'front loaded' nature of family actions. You should not expect any indulgence where tardiness in preparation may cause delay. In many family actions, most of the substantive issues are resolved earlier, rather than later in proceedings. This is achieved through the initial hearings, be they preliminary, procedural, interim or child welfare hearings. Orders granted at early hearings are often the prevailing orders at the conclusion of the case. In other cases, they are of such specific application that they have already been implemented, for example: specific issues orders for a holiday abroad, baptism, change of name, issuing of a passport or attendance at a particular school. Effective advocacy at these hearings can therefore be highly significant.

These general principles set the context in which your advocacy will take place. They will be uppermost in the sheriff's mind and should be at the forefront of yours.

Preparation

Proper preparation is key. The court will expect your submissions to be 'helpful'. This means they ought to be concise, relevant and well founded, whatever issue or motion is being argued before the court. Addressing the court with confidence and courtesy is important but even a competent submission can be derailed if key areas of preparation are overlooked. With experience, your preparations will become less

---

[53] See: Ordinary Cause Rules - Act of Sederunt (Sheriff Court Ordinary Cause Rules) 1993 as amended; in particular, case management procedures have been incorporated into OCR 33 where there is a crave for an order in terms of section 11 of the 1995 Act.
Sheriff Court Adoption Rules – Act of Sederunt (Sheriff Court Rules Amendment) (Adoption and Children (Scotland) Act 2007) 2009; Sheriff Court Practice Notes available at scotcourts.gov.uk; *B v G* 2012 S.C.(U.K.S.C.) 293 and *S v L* 2013 S.C. (U.K.S.C.)20.

time consuming and many, if not all, of the following steps will become second nature.

2. Preliminary matters

Types of action and relevant legislation

It may seem obvious but it is important to be clear as to what type of action is calling and what legislation is engaged. There are many different statutes applicable to children, in a range of actions governed by different regulations, involving different parties. There can be 'overlapping interference' where the arrangements for the care of an individual child are made by means of a section 11 order, a compulsory supervision order and permanence proceedings, simultaneously. Over and above those, additional actions may also be raised concerning that same child. However each of these orders can pertain to separate proceedings involving different parties, calling before different sheriffs. Establish a clear understanding of what litigation is ongoing in relation to the child and what disposals are available to the court.

Types and purpose of hearings

Just as there are many types of actions, it follows that there are many different types of hearings. Due to this multiplicity of actions and unfamiliar terminology, it is often difficult for clients who have received court papers to tell you precisely the type of hearing which has been fixed and its purpose. Similar terminology is used for different types of hearings. Ask the client for all the papers she has received and read them as soon as possible. It is essential to know the purpose of the hearing as it may be a routine hearing in terms of the OCR, or it may be a hearing fixed specifically to address a pressing or contentious issue. If in doubt, or there are no papers, a quick call to the sheriff clerk or your opponent, if known, can assist in identifying the basics. If there is an existing file then it will probably contain the necessary information. The regulations relating to the type of action or legislation will assist further your preparations, as will the relevant Practice Notes.

Arrangements for the hearing

It is wise to check the date, time and location of the hearing in advance, even if this appears clearly marked on the file or papers. Apologising for your late arrival, or having to explain to the sheriff that your client is elsewhere in the building on your instructions, is unnerving and is not the ideal start to your advocacy. It may also be helpful to know which sheriff will be presiding as this may provoke even more detailed preparations and anxiety! It may not always be clear whether or not your client is required to attend the hearing. If in any doubt advise them that they ought to be there. At the very least, this may assist you with your preparations and conduct of the hearing. It will also assist in reporting to the client the outcome of the hearing, especially if it is a disappointing one.

Objectives of the hearing

It is essential to identify the objectives of the hearing. You will already know what triggered the hearing: whether it arises as a matter of routine in terms of the OCR, has been fixed at the sheriff's request for a specific purpose or has been triggered by a party, or all of the above. Hearings can be multifaceted and the sheriff will be keen to deal with as many aspects as possible, as might your client. These factors will inform the objectives and the steps that are required to prepare fully. Ascertain what the OCR require of the sheriff, parties and agents for the type of hearing. Identify any other issues or motions continued to this hearing and establish what new matters your client or your opponent intends to raise and whether these, or opposition to these, require notice to the court or other party.

Substantive preparations – Ask yourself these questions

Do I require to take my client's instructions?

It is neither advisable nor appropriate to conduct a hearing without being satisfactorily instructed by your client regarding the action at large and the matters arising at the hearing. You may conclude that you are already suitably instructed from previous contact with the client or you may be unclear on your client's position. If there is any doubt, ensure that you speak to the client prior to the hearing. If you do not require to seek instructions, it is good practice and a matter of courtesy, to give the client a quick call to confirm that you will be attending on their behalf or to remind them of the hearing.

What might be the consequences and outcomes of the hearing?

Hearings are fixed in the course of an action to assist in identifying the contentious issues live before the court and, where possible, to resolve the dispute at the earliest opportunity. Interim orders may be sought and granted at these hearings. Such orders may establish a new status quo which could assist or hinder your client's long term objectives. Alternatively, procedural or legal issues may require to be resolved which could change entirely the nature of the action or the remedies available to your client. Worst (or best) case scenario, final orders may be made at a child welfare hearing or an evidential child welfare hearing. Therefore the consequences of inadequate preparation at these early stages for you and your client ought to be to the forefront of your mind.

How will I support the motion or the opposition to the motion?

The earlier into proceedings that the case calls, the more likely it will be that the sheriff has limited information about the child, his circumstances and those of the parties. Bear this in mind: the sheriff is less likely to grant a far reaching order if there is little factual basis to support this. (The converse will apply to later hearings: the more the sheriff knows, the more likely he may be to disturb the status quo.) If you act for the pursuer in a section 11 action you, or your colleagues within your firm, may have detailed information regarding the chronology of the case and the compelling basis for the orders sought. However that may not always be the case. Many actions involving children are raised urgently and so fact-finding time will have been limited. Beyond the writ, you and the sheriff may have little information of any substance. If you act for the defender in the action, you are likely to have even less time and less information. In an adoption or permanence case your client is unlikely to have received any papers other than basic *pro forma* intimation documents and may be unable to advise objectively regarding the background to the case.

The extent of your preparations will be determined by the significance of the hearing or orders to be sought at the hearing. Essentially you wish to persuade the sheriff of your client's position. You need to have the tools to hand to do this:

Family and Domestic Relations Advocacy

- a detailed precognition,
- a copy of the papers that are before the sheriff
- affidavits if appropriate,
- other documentary productions, if appropriate case law, if required,
- and **most importantly**, a properly prepared client.

Detailed precognition

The precognition will only be as good as the person taking it. A long precognition may not be a helpful precognition. Some of the key information to focus on will be:

- Properly identifying the parties.
- Jurisdiction - clarified or challenged.
- A simple chronology explaining key serious and recent incidents, (including the date, time and place of incidents).
- Have there been injuries or medical help required?
- Has there been police involvement?
- Are there witnesses to any of this history?
- Was the child present during any of the incidents?
- Has there been a referral to the Children's Reporter?
- Has there been involvement of other agencies, for example, social work, medics or school?
- What precisely are the orders sought?
- The client's reasons why such orders are (un)necessary and in the child's best interests?
- The client's and child's circumstances.
- The suitability of the client for the orders sought
- The client's proposals in relation to the other parties.
- The client's understanding of the child's views.
- The unsuitability of the other parties.
- What allegations or criticisms can your client anticipate from the other parties?

Copy papers

These can be obtained from the court, client or opponent including any reports from other agencies, the curator ad litem or safeguarder. It will take time to obtain these so request them immediately. If reports or other productions are unavailable to you and are likely to be relied upon by agents or the sheriff, you may require to seek a continuation of the hearing in order to be fully prepared and properly instructed. The sheriff requires to balance the potential prejudice to your client with the need to safeguard the welfare of the child. He may insist that the hearing proceed.

Affidavits

The diligent and time consuming preparation of affidavits is of limited value if the sheriff does not have sufficient time in advance of the hearing to consider them, or if your opponent persuades the sheriff that he is being ambushed! Satisfy yourself that the affidavit is necessary, that it is concise and that it will actually assist the sheriff in reaching his decision. Lodge and intimate them in prior to the hearing where possible.

Ensure that you adhere to the rules and Practice Notes applying to affidavits.

Other documentary productions

What are the allegations and averments crucial to the objective of the hearing? There are often documents available to refute an allegation or support an averment, for example, nursery/school reports or attendance print out, medical or social work report, letters from employer, drug/alcohol counsellor or senior community leaders. There may also be police reports, probation records and schedules of previous convictions. One of those documents could be critical in persuading the sheriff in favour of your client's position.

It is not uncommon for your client to wish to use Facebook and text messages as vouching for certain behaviour from the opponent. Do not just refer in general to what your client may have on his phone otherwise he will interpret this as his cue to thrust his mobile towards the bench. Print screen shots and lodge them as productions.

Case law

The relevance or otherwise of case law will be determined by the circumstances. The sheriff will not need to be schooled in the court's considerations and the overarching principles. However, if there is a particularly unique circumstance or point of law, then leading or recent case law ought to be produced to the sheriff clerk prior to the hearing, where possible. It should also be properly referred to in your submissions. The key point that you rely on should be explained.

Most importantly - A properly prepared client

The most skilful and compelling submission about the suitability of your client to care for, or have contact with the child, will carry little weight with the court if the sheriff has observed your client draw a finger across his neck in the direction of the other party whilst you, oblivious, wax lyrical. Clients need to be informed of their role in any hearing they attend as regards achieving their desired outcome. They are, in effect, their own advocates. The client must also be prepared by receiving effective and accurate advice regarding their prospects of success. An informed client will give informed instructions.

Objectivity

It can be very difficult for clients to separate their wishes from the best interests of the child. Clients find it difficult to remain truly objective. Their instructions can be heavily influenced by their own hurt feelings, anxiety, jealousy or powerlessness. Common sense and reasonableness are often casualties of such emotions. The client must be advised of their unconscious bias and educated wherever possible to separate any self-interest from the needs of the child. It is essential that clients are properly prepared in order to prevent these emotions from clouding their judgement. The needs of the adult will not be prioritised over the needs of the child. For instance, proceedings may follow a recent separation where one party has left the family unit. The remaining parent may wish to restrict the absent parent's contact, claiming that he abandoned the child or the family unit. This, of itself, is not a valid argument against contact. The remaining parent needs to aware that, in general, it is in the child's interest to maintain a close and loving relationship with the absent parent. The client ought also to be advised of their obligation to promote and facilitate contact with the absent parent. A sheriff is entitled to draw adverse conclusions if your client maintains a wholly unreasonable stance regarding the arrangements for the child. Whilst it is appropriate to show compassion, if you remain detached and focussed, your client will be more likely to maintain an objective focus on decision making.

Client conduct at the hearing

Dress, demeanour and decorum are all part of the art of persuasion. The client must remain courteous to and cooperative with the court. These hearings can be a very challenging environment: just as your client has had an opportunity to present her position to the court, her opponent will be entitled to do likewise. Your client must be prepared for the reality of attending an acrimonious hearing conducted within the adversarial system. She may be unnerved by her unfamiliarity with the physicality of the court, may be overwhelmed by its formalities or may require to come face to face with an opponent who is a source of distress or anxiety. She must not allow those difficulties to affect her behaviour. Furious head shaking, loud 'tisking', the rolling of eyes, snorts of derision or interrupting will not engender a confidence by the court in her ability to put the needs of the child before her own. Part of your advocacy preparation is to make sure that she understands this.

Realistic expectations

Clients should be given a realistic expectation of the likely outcomes. Do not fill the client with false hope nor allow him to cling to delusions of his remedies and their outcomes. Given the highly emotive nature of child actions, your client should be made aware of the court's objectives at this stage. Some clients will have high expectations of a complete resolution of all matters, in their favour, at the initial child welfare hearing. Be realistic about what is achievable and reset expectations in accordance with likely outcomes. In some cases clients will expect subtle areas of parenting style and preferences to be regulated by the sheriff. This is unlikely. Different styles of parenting, whilst perhaps a matter of significance to your client, cannot be areas of focus by the sheriff, unless the child is being, or is likely to be harmed by such parenting. This can be very difficult for a parent to accept so these are issues best identified early through precognition and addressed outwith the court. Otherwise an overzealous parent may appear to lack insight into the needs of the child.

Conclusion

Preparation is enhanced by anticipation. Anticipate what your opponent may rely upon in support of his position. Anticipate the questions the sheriff may ask. This is best achieved by adopting an objective perspective of the issues to identify any weakness in your argument. Apply your mind to the sheriff's task: what would you need to hear or see to be persuaded?

3.   Advocacy at the hearing

Preliminaries

You've arrived on time at the correct court. Alert the clerk to your presence and advise him of whom you represent and in which case. Provide any productions, affidavits or case law to be relied upon. There may be cases to call ahead of yours and you may require to wait outside if these are confidential. The wait can be lengthy. Do not allow your client to observe you having a right old laugh with your opponent, even if she's very funny. Most clients will view this as disloyal and unprofessional. It is very helpful, however, to identify your opponent and introduce yourself prior to the commencement of the hearing. Some issues might be resolved literally 'at the door of the court' so arrive at least 15 minutes early to allow time for meaningful discussions.

When your case calls, take a seat at the table. Select the correct side of the table! If you are appearing on behalf of the pursuer, applicant or appellant, sit on the sheriff's left otherwise you may embarrassed if advised, by the sheriff, of your error. The clerk has called the case and you may see him pass the process folder up to the sheriff. Wait. The sheriff will gesture when he is ready for you to address him. If you are for the pursuer, applicant or appellant, you will introduce yourself and your opponents, indicating who appears on behalf of which party. Advise the sheriff if parties are present in court.

Bring a structure to the hearing. It is always best to have set out in note form the list of 'housekeeping' or substantive issues and your factual basis in support. This *aide memoire* will ensure an overall structure. Sometimes a very brief outline of the procedure to date, the purpose and objective of the hearing and any motions to be argued will be helpful to the sheriff. Providing an overview will enable the sheriff to prioritise the issues before him. The sheriff may deal with the 'housekeeping' issues first. Speak slowly and clearly. (Bridget's chapters on Body Language and Voice will help here.) Be prepared to be interrupted. A slow pace will give you more time to think on your feet if the sheriff asks questions.

Advocacy on substantive matters

You will wish to move your motion, or await your opponent to do so. A structured approach can be of great assistance to you and the sheriff. Set out all parts of your motion at the beginning – do not do it piecemeal as the sheriff may find that confusing and frustrating. There may be a mix of requests as to orders to be made in relation to the child and the procedure to be followed thereafter. Address each one. Be as concise as possible. It can be difficult to strike the correct balance between relevant detail and a rambling address. The longer the submission, the greater the risk of reaching the tipping point and boring or irritating the sheriff. You may have to address some very serious allegations already contained within in the papers. Be candid: there is a fine line between mitigation and aggravation. The sheriff will often indicate, sometimes quite subtly, that they have heard enough on that point, in which case, move on.

Address the statutory tests and offer reasoned and reasonable information. Make the proposition of what the sheriff ought to do an attractive one. You may invite the court to rely on information provided to you by your client in precognition and discussion, or from your discussions with potential witnesses. The client must be aware of the consequences if he places before the court information which is subsequently shown to be unfounded. This may affect the sheriff's findings as to his credibility and reliability and the consequences of that could be far reaching. You, the solicitor, must never knowingly mislead the court.

As well as the information being accurate, it must also be relevant. It is understandable that your client may wish the court to be advised of his version of the facts and that certain facts be emphasised. It is always necessary to filter information and to select what you believe best supports the arguments you are making. Your client should be involved in that process prior to the hearing to ensure he understands what the court will consider to be the salient issues.

Family and Domestic Relations Advocacy

Having set out what you are asking the sheriff to do and the factual basis for this (including reference to any affidavits or productions) refer the sheriff to the case law if appropriate. Give the sheriff time to retrieve the case from the papers before him. Set out the circumstances of the case and the outcome. Take the sheriff to the applicable paragraphs of the decision and either read them to the sheriff or allow him time to read it to himself. Then tell the sheriff what you wish him to take from the authority and apply in this case. Then tell him the basis for that.

When your submission is concluded, advise the sheriff accordingly and sit down. The sheriff may have further questions or may then hear from your opponent. Note your opponent's submissions and any questions from the sheriff. Often those questions will give an indication of what the sheriff thinks ought to happen. If such comments are favourable, your submissions can be tailored to that line. If the sheriff appears to be favouring your opponent's submissions, your submissions can target the consequences of such orders and potential future problems. The sheriff may revert to you in response to your opponent. If so, concisely respond to the outstanding points with regard to the sheriff's comments. Avoid the temptation simply to repeat your earlier submission. The sheriff is looking for you to offer something new.

Ensure your submissions are measured and reasonable, even where the issues are very serious. Avoid mirroring your client's feelings of panic/ frustration/ fear/ disdain. Your client's perception of immediate risk or fear of long term harm can be conveyed through polite, forthright and considered submissions.

4. Outcome

The sheriff will deliberate and issue his decisions. This may be immediately following submissions, after an adjournment or by way of a Note some days later. If his decisions are issued verbally at the hearing, note these carefully along with the terms of any substantive orders, the date and time of any further hearings and any requirements for agents to comply with meantime.

Reporting to client

It is essential to communicate the outcome to the client, even if she has been present at the hearing. Recap the substantive decisions and reasons for these. Even

Family and Domestic Relations Advocacy

where the outcomes are on the whole favourable to your client, he still may not have absorbed the finer details of some onerous undertaking by him, or some other aspect of the decision favourable to his opponent. If the outcome is unfavourable to your client's position, he may be disappointed and emotional. Initially your client may seek to hold you responsible for an unfavourable outcome. You will have already attempted to manage your client's expectation so remind him of earlier discussions and suggest that a more detailed analysis ought to happen after he has had time to reflect on the day's events.

You should write to your client recapping on the motions and submissions made at the hearing together with the decisions and the sheriff's reasoning. State clearly the orders made and what they mean. Set out a plan for discussions about further actions to follow and timescales for this. In particular, ensure that the client is aware of all obligations upon him and the court's expectations of him.

Recording

Keep your *aide memoire* and notes from the hearing on the file together with any court report *pro forma*. Enter in the court diary and management system any future hearing dates and any deadlines for further work for the progression of the case.

Finally

There is no substitute for experience. Before you begin appearing in court, try to sit in on other hearings wherever possible. This will familiarise you with your local sheriffs and the lexicon of court. Speak to friends and colleagues about their court appearances. You will find that the ones worth listening to have learned more from their mistakes than their successes. Use their experience and advice to avoid some of the errors which will inevitably accompany your first steps in family and domestic relations advocacy.

** **Claire Anne McFadden** is Partner at JK Cameron Solicitors who have a Specialist Adoption and Permanence practice throughout Scottish courts. Claire Anne is an Accredited Specialist in Child Law and oversees all adoption and permanence work at the firm. In the course of each year Claire Anne conducts many contested adoption and permanence order cases as well as conducting other child and family cases and undertaking curator / bar reporter positions on a regular basis. She was the principal solicitor in the Supreme Court case of S v L. She has given evidence at the High Court in London as an expert witness on adoption law in Scotland. Claire Anne regularly provides training and education seminars for solicitors, health professionals and social work services.*

13   FINAL WORDS – A PRACTICE REGIME

"The fight is won or lost far away from the witnesses, behind the lines, in the gym, and out there on the road; long before I dance under those lights."

Muhammad Ali

You may have reached the final chapter of the legal advocacy section, but you have not become a competent advocate simply by reading this far. You did not learn to swim, to drive a car, or to play golf simply by reading about it. There is learned muscle memory involved, and mental effort to forge the distinct neural pathways which will enable you effortlessly to compose non leading questions at will. You need to practise, and practise away from the stress of the courtroom. One way is to practise in a group. Never miss the chance to participate in any mock civil trial. The problem with that is that you will never get enough personal time in the spotlight. The best method of practice is by yourself. You don't need a lot of time to do this, and one of the particular benefits of modern mobile phone technology is that no one will think you unusual because you appear to be talking to yourself. So practise in the car, at home, or whilst out walking. Don't fall for the line that only perfect practice makes perfect. You are not going to be perfect, now or ever. So practise as much as you can squeezing in 5-10 minutes at odd parts of the day. I have outlined three exercise scenarios. Only the third is from a real life case, but that is not the point. The purpose is to habituate and groove the mind and the vocal chords, so that you can run through any witness story examining both in chief and in cross.

Final Words – A Practice Regime

Exercises:

1. The Teddy Bears' Picnic

If you go down in the woods today you're sure of a big surprise
If you go down in the woods today you'd better go in disguise
For every bear that ever there was will gather there for certain
Because today's the day the Teddy Bears have their picnic

Every Teddy Bear who's been good is sure of a treat today
There's lots of marvelous things to eat and wonderful games to play
Beneath the trees where nobody sees they'll hide and seek as long as they please
That's the way the Teddy Bears have their picnic

Picnic time for Teddy Bears
The little Teddy Bears are having a lovely time today
Watch them, catch them unaware and see them picnic on their holiday
See them gaily gad about
They love to play and shout
They never have any cares
At six o'clock their Mummies and Daddies will take them home to bed
'Cause they're tired little Teddy Bears

If you go down in the woods today you better not go alone
It's lovely down in the woods today but safer to stay at home
For every bear that ever there was will gather there for certain
Because today's the day the Teddy Bears have their picnic.

The witness is Mr Edward Bear. You are first of all examining in chief. He attended the picnic the week before. Draw out all the elements in the song from him using only open questions, that is, no leading questions of any kind. Then cross examine Mr Bear, eliciting all the elements in the story but this time using only leading questions. Although this might seem a silly exercise it works well, particularly in a group situation, where the rest of the group is primed to interject the minute any inappropriate method of questioning is used.

Final Words – A Practice Regime

2. Any Sherlock Holmes story

The Adventures of Sherlock Holmes by Arthur Conan Doyle is now free to download from Kindle. Pick a story like ***The Adventure of the Red Headed League.*** Take witnesses through the evidence first of all in chief, for example, examine Dr Watson in chief. You will take from him his personal history and qualifications, his association with Sherlock Holmes, his role in a typical Sherlock Holmes investigation, how he became aware of the particular facts and circumstances of the Red Headed League, and the subsequent unfolding of events. Do the same for the other principal witnesses in the story, for example, Mr Wilson.

Then change to cross-examination mode on the same witnesses on the same facts. Discipline yourself to asking no leading questions in chief, and only leading questions in cross.

3. Case File
Dario Danielli v. Equity Blue Star Limited

> This case is useful for a group or moot litigation exercise. The papers contain examples of reasonably competent examination-in-chief and cross-examination of the defender. There is a report by an expert witness. There are previous statements which can be introduced. There are photographs which can be put to witnesses. There is quite a lot which can be said on both sides. A particular point relates to the tendency of the witnesses to usurp the function of the court by apportioning blame. There is also a useful opportunity to confront the witness Wilson with his statement to the police. You should note that his statement to the police as to blame is inadmissible insofar as his view of fault is of no consequence. However it would be admissible as to show the witness's state of mind immediately after the accident. If he comes up with a version which completely exonerates the pursuer the statement can be put to him to show that he has changed his mind. Assign each participant a witness to examine or cross examine. You will need an adjudicator to act as sheriff. Have other persons make submissions at the end on liability, apportionment of liability and contributory negligence. For those of you who need to know the answer, *Bryce v. McKirdy* 1999 SLT 998 is a case on similar facts.

INDEX OF PAPERS

DARIO DANIELLI v. EQUITY BLUE STAR LIMITED

1. Record

2. Statement by Dario Danielli

3. Statement by Mark Wilson

4. Statement by P.C. Stephen Archibald

5. Report by Angus John Walker, Accident Investigation Specialist

6. Examination and Cross-Examination of Sean McDonnell

1. RECORD
(Personal Injuries Action)

SHERIFFDOM OF TAYSIDE CENTRAL AND FIFE AT KIRKCALDY

DARIO DANIELLI, residing at 29 Glenthorpe Road, Methil, Fife KY8 3BA

PURSUER

against

EQUITY BLUE STAR LIMITED, a company incorporated under the Companies Acts and having their Registered Office and place of business at Liberty House, New Road, Milton Keynes CM14 4GD.

DEFENDERS

The pursuer craves the court —

(a) To grant decree for payment by the defenders to the pursuer of the sum of FIFTY THOUSAND POUNDS (£50,000.00) STERLING.

(b) To find the defenders liable in the expenses of the action.

STATEMENT OF CLAIM AND ANSWERS

Statement 1   The pursuer is Dario Danielli. He resides at 29 Glenthorpe Road, Methil, Fife KY8 3BA. His date of birth is 20th March 1961. He is a shop manager. The defenders are an insurance company with Registered Office at Liberty House, New Road, Milton Keynes CM14 4GD. At the material time, the defenders were the insurers of vehicle registration number SB63 PMU, driven by Sean McDonnell for the purpose of the European Communities (Rights Against Insurers) Regulations 2002. The defenders are directly liable to the pursuer in terms of Section 3 (2) of the said Regulations.

Answer 1   Admitted.

Final Words - *Dario Danielli v. Equity Blue Star Limited*

Statement 2 The court has jurisdiction to hear this claim against the defenders because the pursuer seeks reparation for loss, injury and damage sustained by him through the fault of the defenders. The harmful event in consequence of which the present action proceeds occurred within the sheriffdom of Tayside, Central and Fife at Kirkcaldy.

Answer 2 Admitted this court has jurisdiction.

Statement 3 On 30th July 2013 at approximately 3.00 p.m. the pursuer was working in his fast food takeaway business, Pizza Wow. At the material time the pursuer employed a delivery driver Mark Wilson to do home deliveries to customers. He provided Mark Wilson with a Suzuki Minivan, registration No. SG56 UCV. On 30th July 2013 the engine of the van was overheating. It required to be topped up with water. The pursuer went with Mark Wilson to point out to him the placement of the engine which was located underneath the front passenger seat. The Suzuki Minivan was parked in Bowling Green Street, Methil at its junction with Wellington Road. Bowling Green Street is a two lane undivided carriageway with one lane in each direction. It is a narrow road and at the material time vehicles were parked on both sides of the road. The Suzuki Minivan was parked on the eastbound carriageway in a position facing westerly. The pursuer had to stand in the road and open the passenger door to access the engine. He lifted the front passenger seat. As he was unscrewing the radiator cap to top up the water some steam emitted from the radiator and he took a single step backwards. As he did so a white Lincoln limousine, registration number SB63 PMU driven by Sean McDonnell attempted to pass him. As it did so the limousine struck the pursuer knocking him to the ground. As a result of the accident the pursuer suffered the loss, injury and damage later described.

Answer 3 Admitted that on 30th July 2013 the Suzuki Minivan was parked in Bowling Green Street, Methil at its junction with Wellington

Road; that Bowling Green Street is a two lane undivided carriageway with one lane in each direction; that it is a narrow road and at the material time vehicles were parked on both sides of the road. Admitted that the pursuer was injured in contact with a white Lincoln limousine, registration number SB63 PMU being driven at the material time by Sean McDonnell. Believed to be true that the pursuer had opened the passenger door of the Suzuki Minivan in order to top up the level of the vehicle radiator. The pursuer's personal and business details are not known and not admitted. *Quoad ultra* denied. Sean McDonnell had executed a slow right hand turn from Wellington Road into Bowling Green Street to drop off passengers there. He saw the pursuer leaning in through the passenger door of the Suzuki Minivan. He proceeded slowly and positioned his vehicle as close as possible to the parked cars on his nearside. Sean McDonnell had already driven part of the way past the pursuer when the pursuer suddenly stepped backwards and struck the limousine in the vicinity of the rear offside wheel.

Statement 4 As a result of the accident the pursuer suffered loss, injury and damage. He was in severe pain and was unable to stand up. An ambulance was called and he was conveyed to Queen Margaret Hospital in Dunfermline where he was an inpatient for approximately five days. He suffered an open fracture of the right tibia and fibula. An external fixation device was put in position for four months before being removed. He attended his General Practitioner, Dr Wilson at Love Crescent, Dunfermline who referred him for a course of physiotherapy. He claims damages under the following heads:

i. Solatium
ii. Loss of Income
  The pursuer is the proprietor of the Pizza Wow. He was unable to work for a period of six months following his accident. He required to hire a replacement staff member on a part time basis for a period of six months.

	iii.	Services
		The pursuer required assistance with washing and dressing from his wife Harriet Danielli for a period of around six months or so. A claim is made in terms of S8 of the Administration of Justice (Sc.) Act 1982.
Answer 4		The nature and extent of any loss, injury and damage sustained by the pursuer are not known and not admitted. *Quoad ultra* denied.
Statement 5		The accident was caused by Sean McDonnell's failure to take reasonable care at common law. Reference is made to the Highway Code at paragraphs 180 – 200. The Defenders are directly liable to the pursuer in terms of Section 3(2) of the European Communities (Rights Against Insurers) Regulation 2002, in relation to Sean McDonnell's negligent use of the vehicle.
Answer 5		Sean McDonnell took all reasonable care in the circumstances. The accident was caused by the sole fault of the pursuer. In the event that Sean McDonnell was at fault in any way, the accident was contributed to by the negligence of the pursuer. Denied the action is necessary.

IN RESPECT WHEREOF

Solicitor
AccidentsRus
35 Old Road
Dunfermline
Pursuer's agent.

IN RESPECT WHEREOF

Solicitor for the Defenders
144 West George Street,
Glasgow, G2 2HG

Statement taken: 7th August 2013

2. STATEMENT

By

> **DARIO DANIELLI**, residing at
> 29 Glenthorpe Road, Methil,
> Fife KY8 3BA.
> Tel No: 01333 521678
> Mobile: 07933263800
>
> Date of birth: 20/6/61
> Nat. Insurance No. 410753B
>
> Email address: dario@pzzawow.com

I am currently the owner of Pizza Wow which is a pizza delivery and takeaway situated on Wellington Road, Methil.
I am married with two children aged 16 and 14.
My wife Harriet works in the business as a book keeper.
The business has been in Wellington Road for over 20 years.
Up until around 2005 it was a fish and chip restaurant.
From 2005 I turned it into a takeaway only pizza shop.
I employ a driver, Mark Wilson, to deliver pizzas to customers' houses.
I was involved in a road traffic accident on 30th July 2013.
At that time I had a Suzuki Minivan registration No. SG56 UCV, which Mark used for deliveries.
I normally open the premises at lunch time.
We close at 2.30 p.m. and then open again from 5.00 p.m. until midnight.
When Mark came back in the afternoon he told me that there was a problem with the radiator in the Minivan.
He said that he thought it needed water.
He took a container and went to the vehicle to fill the radiator.
The Suzuki van is unusual in that the engine is directly under the front passenger seat.
I tried to explain this to him.

Final Words - *Dario Danielli v. Equity Blue Star Limited*

However he came back and told me that he couldn't find it.
I decided it would be quicker just to show him.
The vehicle was parked in Bowling Green Street which is just around the side from my shop.
At that time Bowling Green Street was a narrow road which came off Wellington Road.
It was two way at the time.
It is now a one way street.
Cars park on both sides of the road which tends to make it quite a busy street.
I park my van just next to the side door.
It was facing away from Wellington Road down Bowling Green Street, I had to go round to the passenger side which meant I would be standing on the road.
There were parked vehicles on the other side of the road.
I opened the front door, tipped the passenger seat and pushed it back.
I was carrying a kettle full of water.
The cap on the radiator was warm.
I started to slacken off the cap.
I was slowly loosening the cap because I was worried that there would be a blast of steam.
I had my feet in the road and was bending over into the front seat.
Suddenly without any warning I felt a kind of brushing against me.
As I turned round I saw a huge white limousine which then ran over my outstretched right foot.
I hadn't seen or heard it coming.
I banged on the back of the car with my hand.
The driver simply drove on for about 200 yards or so.
I don't think he knew he had hit me.
I was in agony.
I was shouting for an ambulance.
The driver finally came back.
He told me that he didn't know he had hit me and that his passenger had told him to stop.
He didn't apologise or say sorry.
I was later taken to Queen Margaret Hospital in Dunfermline.
I refer to my further statement relating to the injuries suffered and to my financial losses as a result of this accident.
End

Statement taken: 30th July 2013

3. STATEMENT

By

> **MARK WILSON, residing at**
> **99 Kipling Lane, Methil,**
> **Fife KY8 7HU.**
>
> **DOB: 30th June 1975**
> **Tel No: 01333 524789**

My name is Mark Wilson.
I live at 99 Kipling Lane, Methil KY8 7HU.
I currently work as a food delivery driver with Pizza Wow.
I have worked there since July 2011.
I am married but separated.
I have two children aged 10 and 11 from my marriage.
My wife doesn't let me see them.
I currently live with my girlfriend at the above address.
I have known Dario Danielli since July 2011 when I started to work for him.
I should say that this is really just an extra job for me.
I have been on long term sickness benefit.
I get some cash in hand from Dario depending on the number of deliveries.
I am allowed to earn this without it affecting my benefits.
As at 30th July 2013 I had been driving Dario's Suzuki Minivan.
It seemed to me that the radiator was overheating.
I told him so.
The Suzuki van is an unusual vehicle.
I didn't know how to get access to the engine and the radiator.
Dario came out to show me.
The van was parked in Bowling Green Street.
At that time it was a two way street.
There is now a "no entry" sign at Wellington Road meaning that Bowling Green Street is single lane traffic only.

Final Words - *Dario Danielli v. Equity Blue Star Limited*

Dario got a kettle of water and went to the passenger side of the van.
He opened the door.
His feet were in the road.
The road itself is busy and narrow.
There were parked cars on both sides of the road.
Suddenly a limousine came along and ran over Dario's feet.
The driver of the limousine stopped about 200 yards down the road and ran out and came over to us.
He was asking me if Dario was all right.
He didn't apologise.
I am asked about a statement I am supposed to have given to the police.
I don't really recall anything about this.
I am told that I said the driver wasn't to blame.
That is rubbish.
If I said it, it was only because I didn't know how serious the accident was for Dario at the time.
End

Statement taken: 1st September 2013

4. STATEMENT

By

        P.C. STEPHEN ARCHIBALD,
        stationed at Cardenden Police
        Station, Cardenden, Fife KY5 8PC
        Tel No: 01592 690300

I am 25 years old and have 6 years police service.
I have an ordinary driving licence.
I do not have any training or qualifications in accident investigation or advanced driving.
Around 3.15 p.m. on 30th July 2013 I was stationed at Levermouth Police Station.
I was on mobile patrol when I received a call to attend a road traffic incident.
When I arrived I saw that there was a Suzuki Minivan, registration No. SG56 UCV in Bowling Green Street facing down towards Wellington Road.
On attendance we were greeted by Mark Wilson.
He was the only person at the locus.
I now understand that Mr Danielli had been taken to hospital.
I spoke to Mr Wilson and noted a statement as follows:

> "Around 7.00p.m. my boss was filling up the radiator bottle of the van, which was facing down the street. I was watching this from the pavement. A white stretch limo pulled into the street from Wellington Road. As it was passing the van the limo appeared to slow down. When Dario took the radiator cap off steam was rising which caused Dario to jump back and his right leg got caught in the back wheel of the limo. I suspected that his leg was broke. In my opinion the driver was not to blame. It was just an accident. It could have happened to anyone. The driver stopped and provided us with his details."

After we had spoken to Wilson we later noted a statement from Dario Danielli. This was taken at his home on 7th August.

He replied as follows:

"I am the owner of Pizza Wow in Methil. On the night in question I was with Mark on the roadway showing him how to fill the radiator of the delivery van.

As I unscrewed the cap I turned round to the right and became aware of a white limo passing by. I fell to the ground and my right leg was run over by the back outside wheel. About 30 inches from the wheel I banged once on one of the doors. It was an accident although I think the driver should have stopped when I banged. He stopped afterward and gave me his card (Sean McDonnell, Buckhaven, Fife). He apologised. I was in hospital for four days and sustained a broken leg."

Later that same day, we tracked down Sean McDonnell the driver of the limousine. He was initially cautioned under Section 172 and asked to identify the driver of the vehicle.
He replied "I was driving" and signed his reply.
He was thereafter cautioned under terms of Section 1 and Section 3 of the Road Traffic Offender's Act.

He replied to the caution as follows:
"I turned into Bowling Green Street. My passenger came from number twelve. I turned into the street and immediately saw the guy. He was standing next to a delivery van on the roadway leaning into the passenger side with the door closed behind him. I slowed down and gave him a wide berth. I came across to the nearside of the road as far as I could, passed them very slowly then heard a thud and a scream. The guy had jumped back under my rear offside wheel. When I got out the delivery driver had said that the guy had removed the radiator cap and had almost burnt himself and jumped back into the path of the car."

He has again signed this statement at the end.
Both statements were also taken in the presence of P.C. Brown.
Other than checking the offending vehicle and noting no damage to it, we did not carry out any further investigation.
The lack of damage was consistent with the versions given by other witnesses.
I am not exactly certain as to where Dario Danielli would have been standing at the point of impact.

I think the collision would have taken place on the side of the road where his van had been parked, perhaps somewhere towards the centre line.
That however is just guesswork on my part.
No report to the Procurator Fiscal was considered as there was no evidence to support a charge of careless driving.
At the time of the accident I did form the opinion that Dario Danielli was to blame. In my view there was no fault on the part of the limousine driver as there was no evidence that he had been careless.
I do not know how wide the road is nor do I know if there were any parked cards there at the time of the accident.
I did not take dimensions of either the Suzuki Minivan or the limousine.

5. REPORT by Angus John Walker, Accident Investigation Specialist

ANGUS JOHN WALKER

ACCIDENT INVESTIGATION SPECIALIST

REPORT ON ROAD ACCIDENT
WHICH OCCURRED ON
30TH JULY 2013
AT BOWLING GREEN STREET METHIL,
NEAR ITS JUNCTION
WITH WELLINGTON ROAD, METHIL, FIFE

Personal Qualifications

I am a retired police inspector. I have completed 30 years' service. In 2005 was in charge of traffic management for Tayside Police. During my last 25 years of police service I was engaged in solely traffic related matters. I qualified as a police advanced driver in 1980 at the Scottish Police College, Tullyallan. I am a City & Guilds qualified police vehicle examiner. I am a trained accident investigator and hold a Standard Accident Investigation Certificate from Tayside Police having successfully completed a course at Aberdeen University in 2005. I retired from Tayside Police in 2007. Since then I have operated my own consultancy as an Accident Investigator and Traffic Consultant. I have prepared over 250 reports on accidents throughout Scotland. I appear routinely in the sheriff court, in the Court of Session, the County Court in England and the High Court in England. I am a member of the Society of Expert Witnesses.

Basis of Report

This report has been prepared following instructions from Mr Adrian Brigati, AccidentsRus, Solicitors, 35 Old Road, Dunfermline. The following papers and photographs were provided as part of the instructions and which assisted in the preparation of the report:

1. Statement by Dario Danielli dated 7th August 2013.
2. Statement by Mark Wilson dated 30th July 2013.
3. Statement by P.C. Stephen Archibald dated 1st September 2013
4. Copy of court pleadings.
5. Abstract copy of police report.
6. Locus photographs.

Brief Details of Accident

I am advised that Sean McDonnell was driving a white Lincoln Town car, registration number SB63 PMU along Bowling Green Street, Methil towards its junction with Wellington Road, Methil. The Lincoln town car is otherwise known as a stretch limo. It was being driven by Mr McDonnell in connection with his business. He had clients in the rear of the vehicle at the time of the accident. I am advised that the pursuer Dario Danielli is the proprietor of a fast food outlet, Pizza Wow which is located at the corner of Bowling Green Street and Wellington Road, Methil. Whilst he was attending to a mechanical problem in his Suzuki Minivan registration No. SG56 UCV he was standing at the passenger door with it slightly ajar. He was working in the interior under the passenger seat where the engine was located.

It would appear that he turned round and was struck by a glancing blow from the Lincoln Town car. His right foot then appears to have gone under the rear wheel of the Town car. He sustained a fracture tibia.

Observations at the Locus

I visited the locus on 20th December 2013. I ascertained that the local roads authority had made significant alterations to the junction. In particular they had implemented a one way system of traffic flow which was instituted on 15th December 2013. Bowling Green Street runs northeast to southwest and at right angles to Wellington Road which is the major road. Bowling Green Street is narrow with a density of housing on both sides of the road. At the time of my inspection there were parked vehicles on both sides of the street. Bowling Green Street is bordered on the northwest and southeast side by kerb pavements measuring 1.70 metres in width.

Expert Analysis of Available Evidence

The Minivan which was operated by the pursuer is a Suzuki Swift, registration number SG56 UCV which is 1.49 metres in width excluding the wing mirrors. At the material time it was parked at the southeast kerb of Bowling Green Street about 3 metres or so with the junction of Wellington Road and facing down Bowling Green Street. Any vehicle entering Bowling Green Street from Wellington Road would have to make right turn across traffic. The distance from Wellington Road to where the Minivan was parked I measured at 10 metres. The Lincoln Town car is 1.99 metres wide. This measurement excludes wing mirrors. The length of the car can vary depending on the owner's specification. A standard length might be 5.5 metres (18 feet 3 inches). Bowling Green Street is 7.3 metres wide. A family saloon such as a Vauxhall Astra is 1.85 metres wide, a Ford Mondeo motor car is 1.95 metres wide. If not parked hard against the kerb, the allowance should be for say 20cm for a motor car to be parked away from the kerb. The Suzuki Swift Minivan is 1.47 metres wide and applying the same 20cm for its parked position produces a width of 1.87 metres. By totalling the width this produces an available width of channel through which the Lincoln Town car would have to travel. You might also deduct a 40cm for the respective offside wing mirrors of the parked vehicles. This would leave a manoeuvring width of 3.08 metres.

The Lincoln Town car at 1.99 metres plus 20 cm for the wing mirrors produces a potential maximum width of 89cm for this large vehicle to pass or manoeuvre through the parked vehicles. If you were to allow 45 cm (17 inches) on either side of the vehicle it becomes apparent how narrow the potential gap was for the driver of the Lincoln town car.

On the information before me the pursuer was attempting to fix the engine which was located under the passenger seat of the Suzuki Swift Minivan. The offside door was slightly ajar. He stepped backwards and simultaneously turned. He was then struck by an unidentified Lincoln car. The rear wheel passed over his lower leg causing a fracture to the tibia. The Lincoln Town car came to a stop some distance along Bowling Green Street and the driver returned to the locus.

Photographs of the Locus

Photographs (A) and (B) are views of Bowling Green Street with its junction with Wellington Road. They are taken from a position south west of the junction. It can be noted that cars are parked along the pavement on either side of Bowling Green Street. There is a restricted effect when vehicles are parked on both sides of the road. The narrowness of the channel between the respective vehicles would require any driver to proceed with caution and more particularly when driving such a large and lengthy vehicle as the Lincoln town car.

Final Words - *Dario Danielli v. Equity Blue Star Limited*

Any caution being displayed by the driver should increase dramatically if a pedestrian is visible on the road ahead.

The Highway Code

The Highway Code 2007 edition contains rules and instructions to be considered whilst driving. There are a number of relevant rules. In particular:

> Rule 152 about driving in built up areas.
> Rule 205 with regard to pedestrians,
> and in particular Rule 112 about use of the horn.

This states that the horn may be used when "You need to warn other road users of your presence." It advises that it should be used only when your vehicle is moving and never in a built up area between the hours of 11.30 p.m. and 7.30 a.m.

Rule 124 encourages drivers to adapt to driving to the appropriate condition of the road.

Rule 130 which refers to narrow residential streets and advises drivers to drive slowly and carefully in areas where there are likely to be pedestrians.

Rule 181 advises that in urban areas where there is a risk of pedestrians stepping unexpectedly into the road drivers should drive at a speed suitable for the conditions.

Rule 182 advises drivers to drive carefully and slowly when passing parked vehicles.

Rule 92 refers to the use of the horn. It advises that it should be used only when your vehicle is moving and you need to warn other road users of your presence.

The driver of the Lincoln was driving a car of extreme length and considerable width. He was entering into a street the features of which he should have been familiar with. On entry he had an unrestricted view for a distance of at least 50 metres.

He was not confronted with a surprise situation. He advised Constable Archibald: "I turned into the street and immediately saw the guy…….."

It should have been obvious to the driver that a pedestrian was in an extremely vulnerable situation. The simple precaution which should have been taken by the careful and considerate driver should have been a slowing down of the vehicle and a sounding of the horn as it approached, thereby providing due warning to the pedestrian.

It would appear that the driver of the Lincoln slowed down and tried to give the pursuer a wide berth. However, from the measurements this is simply not possible.

Conclusion

The critical factor in this accident is the available road width through which the driver of the Lincoln town car was manoeuvring his vehicle. It is not possible for the reasons stated for the driver to give the pedestrian standing in the position of the pursuer a wide berth. A careful and considerate driver should have realised there was a risk that the pedestrian might move suddenly into the path of his vehicle. He should have sounded his horn.

The Highway Code provides clear advice to drivers when entering such hazardous areas. In the circumstances the driver of the Lincoln vehicle failed to take reasonable care for the safety of the pursuer Dario Danielli.

Angus John Walker.
Accident Investigation Specialist

6. DEFENDERS' PROOF

SEAN McDONNELL (35) sworn –

EXAMINED:

Mr McDonnell, please tell the court your full name? - **Sean McDonnell**

How do you spell your surname? – **M-c-D-o-n-n-e-l-l**

What is your address: - **35 University Avenue, Buckhaven.**

And your age? – **35. I am divorced with two children, aged 5 and 7.**

And your current occupation? – **I am a fire fighter.**

How long have you been with the Fire Service? – **13 years.**

What are your duties as a firefighter? – **I attend at fires when I am called out. Occasionally I drive fire engines as part of my work.**

What if any formal driving qualifications do you have? - **I have an LGV licence.**

What do you mean by LGV? – **Light Goods Vehicle.**

How long have you had an LGV licence? - **I have had an LGV licence for 10 years.**

How long have you had an ordinary driving licence? – **I passed my test when I was 17 so that is 18 years.**

Have you ever been involved in any road traffic accident before the matter in court today?

Objection The issue is not the defenders' driving on previous occasions but on this particular occasion.

Final Words - *Dario Danielli v. Equity Blue Star Limited*

Objection sustained

I now want to ask you about a road accident which occurred on 30th July 2013 in Bowling Green Street, Methil. Do you recall that incident? – **Yes.**

I understand that you were driving a Lincoln stretch limousine along Bowling Green Street? – **Yes.**

Were you driving the vehicle in the course of a business or for something else? – **at that time I had a business where the Lincoln was hired out for special occasions such as weddings and the like.**

On that day did you have passengers with you? – **Yes.**

Who were those passengers? – **The passengers were Jane Morgan and Julie Johnstone.**

And were they known to you? – **Jane Morgan is my married sister and Julie Johnston is my niece.**

What was the trip about? – **It was Julie my niece's birthday that day. I had taken them that day through to Dundee in the morning for shopping, then to Glenrothes for a long lunch, and then home in the afternoon.**

Where did the passengers live? – **They lived in Bowling Green Street, Methil.**

What time of the day was the accident? – **It was around 3.00 pm.**

What was the lighting like at that time? – **It was still daylight.**

What were the weather conditions like? – **It was drizzling.**

Did you turn the vehicle into Bowling Green Street? – **Yes.**

From where had you entered Bowling Green Street? – **from Wellington Road.**

Was that a right hand turn or a left hand turn? – **a right hand turn.**

At that time was Bowling Green Street a one way street or a two way street? – **It was a two way street.**

As you turned into Bowling Green Street did you observe any parked vehicles? – **Yes I saw a Suzuki Minivan.**

As you were entering the street what side was it parked on? - **it was on the right hand side of the street with its front end facing down Bowling Green Street.**

So its back was towards Wellington Road but its front end pointing down Bowling Green Street – **Yes.**

Where was the driver's door? – **the driver's door was next to the kerb.**

Where was the passenger door? – **the passenger door was on the right hand side.**

Were there vehicles parked on the other side of the road? - **Yes.**

Did you observe any individuals around the Suzuki Minivan? – **Yes.**

Please tell the court what you saw as your vehicle entered Bowling Green Street? – **I saw Mr Danielli leaning into his vehicle with the door closed behind his legs and his feet in the roadway.**

At the time did you know what he was doing? – **As far as I was concerned it seemed that he was about to climb into his car.**

Was there anyone else around? – **I didn't see anyone else.**

What did you intend to do at the time? – **I was going to drive about 100 yards down along Bowlilng Green Street and then to drop off the passengers.**

How did you intend to pass the Minivan? – **I had just turned into the road and I was driving slowly. It seemed to me that as long as I took matters carefully there was plenty of room for me.**

What did you do? – **I manoeuvred the vehicle to the far side as close to the gap as I could safely move and proceeded past the Suzuki.**

Is the limousine left hand drive or right hand drive? - **It is an American left hand drive car.**

You were sitting on the left hand side, is that correct? – **Yes.**

How close did you get to the vehicle on your left? – **I was probably about a foot and a half away from the parked cars on the left hand side.**

When you say a foot and a half, do you mean a foot and a half between the side of your vehicle and the parked vehicles, or between the tips of the wing mirrors and the parked vehicles? – **Probably between the tips of the wing mirrors.**

What speed were you going at? – **I estimate about 3 miles per hour.**

Why were you going as slowly as that? – **As you mentioned I have been an LGV driver for almost 11 years and I have worked in the Fire Brigade. I risk assessed the situation. I saw the person standing at the van so I took the appropriate precautions. I slowed down and moved across to my side of the road away from him, observing the hazard as I moved past.**

What clearance were you able to give Mr Danielli in his van at the side? – **As I passed him his van door was fully open. It was at least a foot away from the offside of my vehicle, so the width of the door plus a foot.**

So I take it from that the fact is when the incident happened the door of the Suzuki was open wide?

Objection – leading.

Objection sustained.

At the time you were passing the Suzuki what position was the door in? – **It was wide open.**

And even with it wide open there was a foot or more between the edge of the Suzuki door and the side of your limousine?

Objection – would the solicitor for the defenders please stop giving evidence in the case?

Objection sustained.

What distance would you say there was between the edge of the Suzuki door and the side of your limousine? – **The door was fully open. There was at least a foot of clearance.**

Can I just clarify Mr McDonnell, when you first saw the van and Mr Danielli, was the open door angled or fully open?

Objection – leading. Argued that the question should be allowed as the witness is being given a choice. Objected that it is a false choice. Angled could mean anything

Objection sustained by the court.

By the court – If evidence on important matters is obtained by leading questions I am afraid it is of no value to me.

What was the angle of the door in relation to the Suzuki Minivan when you first saw it? – **I would probably say it was at about 60 degrees or so.**

Can you say whether or not it remained at that angle throughout the incident? – **no when he jumped back the door was fully opened.**

Can you please describe what happened, taking it very slowly? – **As I told you on my right hand side there was a Suzuki van and a person leaning inside the van. I took appropriate measures. I risk assessed the speed and moved across to the left hand side of the road and continued to pass.**

What happened next Mr McDonnell? – **I observed the hazard and continued to pass. I was passing the van looking in the mirror. I observed Mr Danielli was remaining where he was and next thing all I seen was the van door springing open**

Final Words - *Dario Danielli v. Equity Blue Star Limited*

and a thud on the rear offside of the car.

What did you do when you saw that? – **I stopped the car immediately.**

What does immediately mean? – **I think within about 5 or 6 feet.**

Did you get out?

Objection – leading.

Objection sustained.

What did you do at that point? – **I got out right away.**

After you got out what did you do? – **I moved round to the rear of the car and I saw Mr Danielli sitting on the ground holding one of his legs.**

It has been suggested that you didn't stop right away but drove on a couple of hundred yards or so? – **No that is definitely not correct. I should say that when I got out I saw a person I now know to be Mr Wilson who was helping Mr Danielli.**

And when you observed that Mr Wilson was attending to the situation you drove on to your passengers' home. Is that correct?

Objection – leading.

Objection sustained.

What did you do when you observed Mr Wilson attending to this situation? – **I went back to the limousine, drove down 100 yards or so and dropped the passengers off. I then walked back. Can I ask a question?**

By the court: No, it is your solicitor who is asking the questions.

After the accident what if any discussion did you have with Mr Danielli? – **I didn't have any discussion with him. He seemed in a lot of pain.**

What if any discussion did you have with Mr Wilson? - **I spoke to Mr Wilson at that time.**

What did he tell you? – **He told me that Mr Danielli was on the passenger side working with the radiator filler cap for the Suzuki van.**

By the court: Please speak slowly, Mr McDonnell.

He told me the van had been overheating and that Mr Danielli had a kettle to put water into the radiator, that he had removed the cap and suddenly there was a blast of steam.

Mr Cameron: - M'Lady, none of this was put to Mr Wilson in his evidence this morning. If there is to be new material on this issue, it should have been put to Mr Wilson

By the court: I think that's right Mr Grieve. We will hear what the witness has to say but I do wonder what value it can have if it was not put to Mr Wilson. I will allow this to continue under reservation. Could you repeat the question?

What did Mr Wilson tell you - **Mr Wilson said he jumped back because of the blast of steam.**

It might be suggested to you Mr McDonnell that it would have been prudent for you to have sounded your horn before passing Mr Danielli. What do you say about that? – **I had taken the appropriate risk assessment of the situation so far as I was concerned. It seemed to me he was about to climb into the vehicle. I was going at a very very low speed.**

What do you mean by risk assessment? – **Well in the Fire Brigade we take risk assessments all the time. It simply means that you are assessing the hazards in the situation and taking steps accordingly.**

Mr Danielli seemed to you to be in the process of climbing into his vehicle? – **Yes.**

Was there anything to suggest to you that he might suddenly jump back out of his vehicle? – **no nothing at all.**

Final Words - *Dario Danielli v. Equity Blue Star Limited*

Thank you Mr McDonnell, if you just wait there my friend Mr Cameron may have some questions for you.

CROSS-EXAMINED: *(Defender's Proof)*

Good morning Mr McDonnell – **Good morning.**

You had to make a right turn from Wellington Road into Bowling Green Street, didn't you? - **Yes, that's right.**

This would mean cutting across oncoming traffic in Wellington Road, wouldn't it? - **Yes, that's right.**

Did you have to give way to traffic? - **I can't remember if I did or not.**

In any event you told the court that you turned slowly into Bowling Green Street? – **Yes that's right.**

You estimated that your speed was about 3 mph or so? – **It would be about that, I wasn't looking at the speedometer. I knew I had to go slowly.**

And there were parked vehicles on both sides of Bowling Green Street, weren't there? – **Yes.**

You could see that immediately? – **Yes.**

The Lincoln is a left hand drive car isn't it? – **Yes.**

Most UK cars are right hand drive, aren't they? – **Yes.**

But you had no trouble seeing the vehicles in Bowling Green Street on your right hand side – **Not really.**

The vehicles were visible to you as you started your turn into Bowling Green Street? – **Yes, that's right.**

And you would see Mr Danielli as soon as you started to turn in, wouldn't you? — **Yes I saw him right away. I thought he was getting into the car.**

He was on the passenger side wasn't he? — **Yes.**

The Suzuki Minivan is a left hand drive vehicle isn't it? — **Yes.**

When you saw him he had both feet on the ground didn't he? — **Yes.**

His feet were in the road weren't they? — **Yes.**

The upper part of his body was in the van wasn't it? — **Yes it was.**

We have heard evidence that the width of the Lincoln was around 2 metres. That's about right isn't it? — **Yes, if you say so.**

We have heard evidence that when there were parked vehicles in Bowling Green Street the clearance on either side was only about a foot or so. Would you agree with that? — **I would say it was a bit more. The Suzuki Minivan wasn't parked completely in the road. It had been bumped up onto the pavement. So there was a wider clearance on that side.**

Are you telling the court that the Minivan wasn't completely in the road but partly on the pavement? — **Yes.**

Did you give your own lawyer this information? — **Yes, I think so. Maybe not, he never asked me.**

Do you understand that this is the first time that this suggestion has emerged in the case? — **I don't know what you mean.**

Well you heard Mr Danielli give evidence, nobody suggested to him that this Minivan was bumped up onto the pavement, did they? — **I don't know, I just know where it was at the time.**

Final Words - *Dario Danielli v. Equity Blue Star Limited*

On any view, Mr McDonnell you are talking about a very tight squeeze? – **Yes, that's why I had risk assessed the situation and knew that I would need to proceed slowly and with care. I am used to driving a fire engine. I know how to handle a large vehicle. I am risk assessing all the time in my daily job.**

A risk assessment involves three things Mr McDonnell doesn't it? – **I don't know what you mean.**

Well the first point is the nature of the hazard? – **Yes, that's right.**

The second point is the likelihood that the hazard might eventuate? – **Yes, that's right.**

And the third point is the seriousness of the consequences if the hazard does eventuate. Would you agree with that? – **Yes all of that's standard.**

Can I suggest to you that the most important hazard in this situation was the possibility that your car might hit a pedestrian? – **Well I just knew it was a tight squeeze.**

Well the worst that could happen on the other side would be that your vehicle would be scratched, isn't that right? – **Yes.**

And it is more important not to harm a pedestrian than to worry about a scratch, isn't it? – **There would have been no harm done to the pedestrian if he hadn't jumped back.**

Well we may come to that Mr McDonnell but could I ask you to answer the question which was that the most serious hazard confronting you was the possibility that you might hit a pedestrian? – **Yes I knew that. I had no idea he was going to move. You tell me what you would have done in the circumstances.**

I am sorry Mr McDonnell but I can't get involved in a conversation with you. I am only allowed to ask you questions. Your own lawyer can clear up any matters after you have answered my questions.

You were in court when the road traffic expert gave evidence, weren't you? – **Yes.**

You heard him say that the distance from the crown of the road in Wellington Road to where the parked Minivan was, was about 10 metres or 30 feet or so. So for you to come into contact with Mr Danielli, the Lincoln would have to travel at least 30 feet? – **I suppose that's right.**

And you were watching him all the time, that's what you told the court, wasn't it? – **Yes, I was keeping an eye on him.**

Would you take it from me, Mr McDonnell, that 3 mph equates to $4^{1/2}$ feet per second? – **I don't know, I've never worked it out.**

Well it is a matter of arithmetic Mr McDonnell, but for the purposes of my question would you accept from me that it is right? – **Okay, if you say so.**

On your own evidence Mr Danielli was in your full view for at least 5 or 6 seconds? – **I don't know, I wasn't counting.**

You told the court you thought he was getting into the car? – **Yes that's what I thought.**

But he was in your full view for 5 or 6 seconds and didn't get into the car, did he? - **No.**

He was on the passenger side and there was no one on the driver's side, was there? – **No.**

And throughout that time he made no movement to get into the car did he? – **No.**

You must have realised that he was not in fact getting into the car to be a passenger, was he? – **I don't know what he was doing, if he had stayed where he was there would have been no accident.**

You must have realised that it was every bit as likely that he would have stepped back away from the car as get into it? – **He jumped right back. I had no idea that would happen.**

We are not talking about an extraordinary event here Mr McDonnell, we are talking about someone stepping back from a parked vehicle aren't we? – **I told you already he didn't step, he jumped back suddenly.**

The fact is that you had plenty of time to see him didn't you? – **Yes I saw him.**

You knew that he wasn't getting into the car, didn't you? – **I have already told you that I thought he was getting into the car.**

You weren't really sure he knew you were there were you? –

Objection – how can this witness answer as to the state of mind of the pursuer?

Objection sustained.

Well you didn't make eye contact with him did you? – **I can't remember.**

You told us in your evidence that the Lincoln is a quiet vehicle didn't you? – **Yes it's quiet.**

You must have known that there was a chance that Mr Danielli didn't know you were there? – **How could he miss me?**

One thing that you could have done was to sound your horn as you entered Green Street – **I didn't think it was necessary to sound the horn. I don't like sounding the horn in built up areas. It always gives people a fright. If I had sounded the horn there would have been every chance that he would have jumped back or done something silly.**

But you could have sounded the horn well before you reached him, couldn't you? – **No.**

You are familiar with the Highway Code aren't you? – **Yes, everyone is.**

Let me read to you what Rule 112 says about use of the horn. This states that the horn may be used when "You need to warn other road users of your presence."

It advises that it should be used only when your vehicle is moving and never in a built up area between the hours of 11.30 p.m. and 7.30 a.m.

Let me read to you what Section 142 says – reads terms of Highway Code. That's what you could have done, wasn't it? – **I could have done it but I didn't see any need.**

That's what you should have done wasn't it? – **I suppose with hindsight I could have done it but I didn't think there was any need at the time.**

Objection – It is not for this witness to answer what should have been done. That is the issue before the court.

Objection sustained.

Can I reframe the question Mr McDonnell. Say you were to find yourself in that situation tomorrow you would sound your horn as you entered Bowling Green Street, wouldn't you? – **If you say so, I suppose I might.**

By the court – Any re-examination, Mr Grieve?

No re-examination My Lady (in dismissive a tone as possible).

PART TWO by Bridget McCann

INTRODUCTION

Why did I want to write my part of this book?

I work with many young lawyers and I've become increasingly aware of how many skills are needed in the legal world. Many of the 'soft' skills are the ones which cause the most anxiety but get the least attention. These skills sometimes arrive with time but how many nail biting moments, sleepless nights and dry mouths have to be got through before time spent in court eases the experience?

Through my training on the Advanced Advocacy Skills courses at Strathclyde Law School I know what a little guidance and focussed techniques can achieve. I have learned, from my own experience in public speaking and theatre, even the most awkward nervous law student can blossom and feel hope that they too can have the right air of gravitas and assurance required to persuade those watching in court that they are up to the job.

We live in a world which still expects the skills of the Victorian advocates, and yet this generation has had little or no experience in these skills. Few schools offer debating clubs, there is less 'reading out loud' around the class, we are all surrounded by fast speech and there is much more informality generally in the way we deal with each other. Yet suddenly the law graduate is expected to take on the mantle of previous generations and acquit him or herself with the style of these previous generations.

Most students or newly qualified lawyers realise that a few hours is not enough to embed what they've just learned with me and they often ask if I can suggest a book to reinforce and remind them of the techniques I teach. There are libraries full of

Introduction

books, usually designed to be read by actors, on posture, relaxation and voice but I felt that these weren't specific enough to the needs of the court practitioner.

The aim of writing this section of the book is to help you to feel, look, sound and ultimately *be* more confident. There are 8 chapters, which should be worked through in the order in which they appear here. There are exercises in each section and it is these exercises that will transform you if you put in the time. If you are serious about your profession, five or ten minutes a day will make all the difference.

You should try all the exercises to see what works best for you, then incorporate them into a brief daily routine. Actors work on their voices for years when training, and continue to refine their vocal skills for the rest of their lives. I am going to suggest that you do likewise. Being a lawyer is not simply a career, it is a vocation. I know that you don't have the time to spend hours each day working on your vocal skills. But you will be amazed at the incremental gains, and then at the substantial progress you will make if you commit to a regular practice routine. I am afraid there are no shortcuts. I have a brief Advocacy Quick Start section which you can use each morning before court. I have also selected a set of exercises for an Advocacy Core Practice Routine, with accompanying QR inserts. The Advocacy Core Practice Routine should take you no more than 10 minutes a day.

I've tried to explain each exercise as clearly as I can but as this whole business of walking into a court, standing, sitting and speaking, is largely physical, I've inserted QR codes which will take you to a short film on YouTube, where you can see and hear how the exercise works. All you need is the QR app on your smart phone to access these training films. (These are also available on my website www.bridgetmccanntrainer.com.) These films can be found in the individual chapters as they arise but are also collated at the end of the book under the chapter headed 'Exercises' so that once you understand the *why* of an exercise you can skip that and just work on the exercise itself.

Every so often, when training, I've seen something that makes it all worthwhile: it's that moment when I see a nervous diffident speaker suddenly 'get it'. They get what it's all about. The joy of relishing our wonderful language, delivering it with aplomb and holding the audience in the palm of their hand. That feeling is within your grasp too. Good luck.

14 ANXIETY

"All I could think was that the sheriff could see that my hands were shaking so much that I could hardly hold the papers."

In all my years of training, there is one subject which comes up the most as the key area of concern for those of you appearing in a courtroom: anxiety. 90% of all people I coach have come to me because their performance anxiety is causing them sleepless nights, illness and even a desire to change jobs after their hard won qualifications.

In this chapter I'll be looking at:

- Understanding 'Fight or Flight'
- How to get on top of 'Fight or Flight'

UNDERSTANDING 'FIGHT OR FLIGHT'

Everyone experiences performance anxiety. However, it is the *degree* to which it affects you that is important. Many people are adversely affected by too much anxiety which bedevils them in many negative ways, all of which are detrimental to them performing at their best in court.

I'm going to take some time to explain 'Fight or Flight' as it is commonly called. Understanding why you have these crippling symptoms of anxiety is important if you want to overcome them.

There is also very little point in working on any other of the areas I teach, such as posture, breathing and voice unless the speaker has control over his or her mental and physical state.

Whenever you doubt your ability to perform in court you are opening yourself up to the possibility of being overcome by 'stage fright'. In other words, the mental and physical go hand in hand. You may be saying to yourself "I can't do this", or "I've previously appeared before this judge and it went badly" and the body then kicks-in to protect you from the threat of appearing in court.

So what is 'Fight or Flight' or Performance Anxiety? It is the body's physical and mental response to a threat. The most common *physical* symptoms include:

- Tension
- Shaking
- Increased heart rate
- Nausea
- Sweating
- Dry mouth

The most common *mental* symptoms include:

- A feeling of being out of one's body
- Feeling panicky
- Having negative thoughts
- One's mind going blank

At its extreme it manifests itself as stage fright, literally rendering the speaker useless. Importantly, although perhaps less critically, it can reduce the impact of a performance.

The list of symptoms is much longer, but even these few symptoms can work *against* the lawyer in court who needs to think on his or her feet and portray a calm professionalism.

Some people are so overcome by 'Fight or Flight' that they change professions and deploy tactics to avoid the situations that bring on the worst of their anxiety. However, understanding that this is a normal emotion and that there are ways of combating it means that with some practice and knowledge, even the most nervous of 'performers' can overcome their dread and move on successfully.

Anxiety

So what is 'Fight or Flight'? It is our body's primitive, automatic, inborn response that prepares the body to 'fight' or 'flee' from perceived attack, harm or threat to our survival.

When our fight or flight response is activated, certain hormones like adrenalin and cortisol are released, speeding the heart rate, slowing digestion, shunting blood flow to major muscle groups and changing various other autonomic nervous functions giving the body a burst of energy and strength. Our pupils dilate. Our awareness intensifies. Our sight sharpens. Our impulses quicken. We become prepared—physically and psychologically—for fight or flight.

Unfortunately, these responses, which saved us when we were primitive man faced with a sabre-toothed tiger, are the same responses that our body experiences when faced with a challenging or even patronising judge although there is no *physical* danger!

We know this consciously, but the instinctive part of our brain hasn't caught up yet with human progress and responds to stress by triggering our bodies to fight or flee from the sabre-tooth tiger that isn't there.

In most cases today, once our fight or flight response is activated, we cannot flee. We cannot fight. We cannot physically run from our perceived threats. When we are faced with modern-day sabre-toothed tigers, we have to stand in the courtroom and "control ourselves."

What are the negative consequences in terms of appearing in court? In this fight or flight state we are excitable, anxious, jumpy and irritable. With trembling hands and a pounding heart, we find it difficult to execute precise, controlled skills (have you ever wondered why you can't even seem to turn the pages in your notes?). The intensity of our focus on survival interferes with our ability to make fine judgements based on drawing information from many sources. We find ourselves less able to make good decisions.

When the perceived threat is gone, our systems are designed to return to normal function via the *relaxation response* but in our times of chronic stress this often doesn't happen enough. Every time your body triggers the fight or flight response, for situations that are not life threatening, you are experiencing a false alarm. Too many false alarms can lead to stress related disorders such as:

- Heart disease
- Irritable bowel syndrome
- High blood pressure
- Headaches
- Immune system disorders
- Insomnia

That is the long-term outcome of unnecessary 'fight or flight'. The short-term effects were outlined at the top of this chapter.

How to get on top of 'Fight or Flight'

Breathing

Breath provides a direct route for accessing and channelling this powerful instinct. Deep diaphragmatic breathing is the answer and activates the relaxation response.

If your breath isn't sufficiently centred, your unconscious mind simply will not reverse the negative thoughts which brought on the fight or flight response. This is because the shallow breathing pattern and physical tension created by the nervous 'flight' state ensures that the brain keeps flooding the system with stress hormones.

A shallow, rapid breathing pattern and physical tension occur spontaneously when we are under pressure in order to help us make a quick escape and physically protect ourselves if necessary. This is a primitive response to danger not intended to help us take the space in the courtroom, or on the platform, with dynamism, charisma and expertise. Centring the breath, however, begins to reverse that stress cycle because the muscle memory of a centred breath is linked to confidence and ease. Breath and mind-set can then work together to create success.

Ideas arrive with an intake of breath, so holding our breath can prevent new ideas from forming. When we hold our breath the unconscious mind engages entirely in the effort of trying to make us breathe again.

Anxiety

I have seen examples of presenters or advocates freeze when a tough question has been put to them. Freezing is also part of the protective response. (Some animals, such as lions, fight, others such as horses, flee, and then there are those such as rabbits that hold their breath in the undergrowth.) I then see these recipients instinctively suck in their diaphragms almost as if a sharp object hits them in that area. If they then fail instantly to centre the breath, this answer is likely to sound uncertain, the voice may even crack because there is no breath to support it, and the shallow 'flight' pattern breathing will give them unconfident body language. When they leave the courtroom and their breath naturally centres, a more effective answer is likely to come flooding back.

Try out some of the breathing exercises mentioned in the 'breathing' section. Start to become aware of what is happening to your body when stressed and learn to relax the areas where tension has crept in.

The key exercise to use from the chapter on Breathing is:

The Flower and the Candle QR

Relaxation

Relaxation can be done on a daily basis and will have the effect of generally reducing your stress levels. This is useful in the lead-up to the start of an important case which is when anxiety tends to increase. You may suffer from insomnia as the case and all the facts go round and round your head, making it impossible for you to switch off.

There are some suggested exercises in the chapter on Relaxation. You might also want to look long term at yoga, tai chi, meditation and massage.

Avoiding caffeine
Caffeine triggers the fight or flight response and stays in the body for up to 18 hours. It really is best avoided especially if you already feel anxious.

Anxiety

Think about your client
I've seen nervous young lawyers, overcome with anxiety, change completely when reminded that they are speaking on behalf of their client. That resolve to speak up on behalf of someone else mentally changes their attitude and allows them to cope.

Turn the camera off you
Another way of deflecting anxiety is to imagine that there are two cameras in the courtroom. One of them is focussing on you and the other is facing towards the activity around you. I'd like you to imagine that you can turn off the camera that is focussing on you. (We all feel self-conscious when we focus on ourselves.) All that is left is the outward facing camera. You will find, if you can pay more attention to what is going on around you, that you will feel less self-aware and anxious.

Perceive it as a challenge
First of all we need to accept that some performance anxiety is necessary. Without the thrill of some nerves, there can be the danger of flatness. There needs to be a balance between adrenalin and relaxation to create focus and clarity of mind.

Let's look at what the brain can do to counteract this performance anxiety

If you think of speaking in court as a threat, you will experience anxiety. However, not everything in life needs to be black and white. You wouldn't have chosen a career in court if there weren't some aspects of it that you found satisfying and pleasurable. If the negative aspects have taken over, then it's time to redress the balance.

How stressed someone feels depends on how much damage they think the situation can do them and how closely their resources meet the demands of the situation. It may involve other people's opinions of us, our career prospects and even our own values.

It might be useful to change one's interpretation of stressful situations, thereby reducing the perception of threat.

Have you considered looking at the whole experience as a challenge rather than a threat? Instead of thinking any of the following:

Anxiety

- I don't think this will go well.
- I made a mess of this last time.
- I feel too anxious.
- I don't know what I'm doing.

Why not decide to take a different viewpoint such as:

- I've studied for years to get to this point and I know my stuff.
- I'm thoroughly prepared for this case.
- It didn't go so badly last time really.
- I will enjoy achieving success.
- I've chosen this career and I'm one of the lucky ones to be able to live out my dream.

This only works if you really believe in the positive thoughts. If you are just going through the motions, your brain will not be deceived and the 'fight or flight' syndrome will win.

We 'talk' to ourselves all through the day and it may be that negative chat dominates without us being aware of it until it becomes the default position. Often the negativity springs from some event in the past. You may have had a minor attack of nerves in court early in your career, but over time this episode has grown until, in your mind, you tell yourself that you are petrified every time. Thus your internal conversation could be: "I'm too nervous to appear in court. I'm no good at this. I let myself down every time I appear." You could review the situation and be kinder to yourself. Tell yourself that you were nervous once, but that was understandable, forgive yourself and then move on.

What you want to do is to change negative self-talk into positive self-talk

You may still have the same physiological responses but those too can be viewed in a more positive light. So let's say, when nervous, you feel more aware of your heart beating faster. Negative self-talk would translate that to mean that you were too anxious to perform well. However, positive self-talk can translate it to mean something exciting. You could say in your self-talk: "I'm about to step out of my comfort zone. How exciting! Let's see how this goes!"

Remember a time when things went well for you in a similar situation. Bring to mind how you felt emotionally and physically. Use the memory of this occasion to re-live those feelings. Hold on to how this made you feel and carry that with you to give yourself confidence.

Research has shown that simply *thinking* a negative thought produces physiological changes in the body. That's how powerful thoughts are.

And finally

Let's end this chapter on a positive note. It seems that the instinctive fight or flight phenomenon is responsible for most of the greatest acts of heroism that we can imagine, like firemen plunging into blazing buildings to rescue people and mothers finding the strength to lift their children from under crashed cars. So, use the fear.

15 RELAXATION

"My jaw was so tense I could hardly speak. My knees seemed to be so locked that I could hardly walk to the lectern."

Everyone wants to look and sound confident in court. Learning how to be relaxed is a useful skill.

In this chapter I'll be looking at:

- Why it's important to overcome tension
- How to identify where you hold tension
- Suggested relaxation exercises

Why it's important to overcome tension

Before I talk about how to use relaxation to prepare you for appearing in court I'm going to talk about first impressions. You'll get the connection in a minute.

We like dealing with people whom we like and trust and think are competent. Have you considered that by not being relaxed, you could be adversely affecting how people feel about you?

It takes only one tenth of a second for us to make up our minds about people, according to research published recently at Princeton University.[54]

---

[54] Janine Willis and Alex Todorov. Princeton University. *Psychological Science Volume 17. No 7.* Research Article: *First Impressions. Making Up Your Mind After a 100-Ms Exposure to a Face.*

They found that people made judgements about the attractiveness, likeability, trustworthiness, competence and aggressiveness of other people after looking at their faces for 100 milliseconds.

During the experiment it was also discovered that longer glances at the same faces caused people to become more convinced of their initial opinions.

It can take 5 or 6 return visits to change initial preconceptions.

Like it or not, judgements based on facial appearance play a powerful role in how we treat others, and how we in turn are treated. Psychologists have long known that attractive people get better outcomes in practically all walks of life. People with "mature" faces receive more severe judicial outcomes than "baby-faced" people; and having a face that looks competent (as opposed to trustworthy or likeable) may matter greatly as to whether a person gets elected to public office.

Now there might not be much that we can do about our looks but there is no doubt that tension caused by anxiety doesn't bring out the best in anyone. Any of the character traits listed above from the Princeton experiment can be skewed or altered through tension – nervous tension can make someone look impatient or shifty and suggests or betrays a lack of self-confidence or conviction. Nervous tension can stop someone looking trustworthy because of anxious facial tics and darting eyes, as well as physical restlessness. And so on.

Another negative side to being tense is the effect you have on those around you. It is difficult for them to feel relaxed in your company.

With this recent research in mind, as well as understanding 'fight or flight', it is worth addressing physical tension. We all know when we are told to relax that it's almost the last thing we are able to do but somehow we need to find ways to reach a level of relaxation that will allow us to perform at the professional level expected of us.

How to identify where you hold tension

The easiest way is to become more aware of your body and work with it away from the court. Learning physical relaxation will help you to recognise how your body responds to stress. You will become aware of the feeling of relaxed muscles and

Relaxation

tense ones. You will begin to recognise when tension creeps in and then address it. This really means that you need to do relaxation exercises on a regular basis.

Where do you hold tension? QR

We all favour certain parts of our bodies to hold the worst of our tension. A good way to find out what happens to your body when in a stressful situation is to work through the 'body check'. Write down all the parts of the body from the feet upwards on one side of a sheet of paper. You will then need to ask a friend or partner to sit with you and call out these parts in turn and write down any comments you make as they do so, opposite each listed part of the body. The first step is to sit down comfortably and put yourself back in a situation which you remember as being very stressful.

As your partner calls out the parts of your body, just say what comes into your mind. This is not a technical exercise. You may want to say things such as 'my feet are curled tightly', 'my thighs feel tight', 'I can feel my jaw clenching' and so on. Then have a good look and assess what happened to your body during that stressful episode. It's very likely that to a greater or lesser degree this is the way your body *always* reacts. Obviously, if you discover that your jaw is clenched, your tummy sucked in and your thighs are tense, this is not going to help you look and sound assured in court.

Now go back to that comfortable chair, close your eyes again and this time think of a moment when you were happy and relaxed, and call out your thoughts and memories against the same parts of the body. You should have a different vocabulary! 'My face feels loose', 'my legs feel heavy' and 'my shoulders are down' for example.

Only you can interpret this reading of your body. It may be that you only hold tension in a few places and you are already aware of them. You may have some surprises. You may also be horrified to discover that you hold tension nearly everywhere.

The usefulness of this exercise is that you are on track to a better understanding of your body.

Relaxation

Don't forget that, wherever you hold tension, it creates a knock-on effect so *any* tension creates problems. If even clenching your feet affects the sound of your voice, consider what holding tension in your shoulders can do.

Suggested relaxation exercises

These exercises need to be done somewhere quiet. Allow some time so that you really start to connect to your body in order to become aware of how it feels to be totally relaxed. Some of these exercises will only take a minute or two and others considerably longer. Pick and choose to fit in with your life and work.

- Go back to your list of the parts of the body and this time consciously tense and relax each of them in turn. Some of you may already shake out tension or release tension in the shoulders before appearing in court, but I'm fairly certain that you will be missing out other areas which will be tense and which will give you away. Be thorough.

- Lie on the floor, knees up, with the soles of your feet flat on the ground. Check for tension and try to release it. Unclench your jaw. Try doing nothing except breathing. Focus on imagining that the breath is coming from your diaphragm. Concentrate on the *out* breath and allow the *in* breath to take care of itself.

   (You can also do this exercise but with your calves supported on a chair. This position helps to open up the breath.)

   General Relaxation QR

- Stand with your feet shoulder-width apart. Knees and thighs should be soft. Raise your arms above your head and stretch towards the ceiling, without lifting your feet off the floor. Hold this for 20 – 30 seconds and then imagine that you are a puppet and someone is cutting the strings, first at the wrists and then at the shoulders so that your arms flop down by your side, feeling heavy. Now the string supporting your head is cut and the weight of your head makes it flop down falling forward bringing the back with it until you are bent over.

Relaxation

- Now bend your knees and just hang there with heavy head and arms. Hold this position for a short while, remembering to breathe, and then gently unfold, vertebra by vertebra, until you are upright again. The trick to this exercise is to take your time.

- Lie or sit in a comfortable position and close your eyes. Now imagine you are sitting beside a warm fire or lying on a deserted beach in the sunshine. Concentrate on your breathing and as you breathe out say to yourself "I'm letting go" or "I feel calm".

- Yawning and stretching help to release tension and to stimulate energy.

- Gently slapping yourself all over especially in the areas of tension is helpful.

- Book regular massage sessions so that you start to become familiar with feeling totally relaxed.

QR Tension in the face

- Reduce tension in the face to facilitate clear speech by scrunching up your face as if it were a fist, closed and tight, and then open the whole face by pretending that you are extremely surprised, opening your eyes and mouth wider than normal. Repeat a couple of times.

- Physical exercise, even just standing up and walking around, is calming.

- Mindfulness meditation. (This meditation helps you to change the way you think, feel and act by using a combination of breathing techniques, meditation and living in 'the moment'.)

16 BREATHING

"Sometimes in court I literally run out of breath in the middle of my speech."

I discussed earlier the importance of breathing in terms of controlling anxiety. It's also vital in public speaking because the breath powers the voice. It's as simple as that.

In this chapter I'll be looking at:

- The mechanics of breathing
- How to use breathing to control 'fight or flight'
- How to use the breath to support speech

The mechanics of breathing

We all take breathing for granted but it is useful to be familiar with the mechanics of breathing so that we can understand why breathing sometimes lets us down, especially when we are nervous.

Literally half of your body is involved in breathing. The key areas are the rib cage, the diaphragm and the abdomen. You see that I haven't mentioned the lungs. That is because they are, to all intents and purposes, passive. It is the surrounding muscles that do the work – the diaphragm and the intercostal muscles. Many people, when asked to take in a big breath, lift their shoulders with great effort but in fact this only results in the opposite outcome to what is required, giving your lower ribs less room to open and thereby reducing the amount of breath that is taken in.

So it is helpful to stop thinking of the upper chest when thinking of breathing. I

Breathing

find it helpful to start to focus on the abdomen, to imagine that my mouth is in my belly. Straight away I find that this leaves my throat and shoulders free from tension and, as I have explained in previous chapters how tension adversely affects the voice, this is a helpful start to having a more relaxed voice.

I am now focussing on my belly. Why? Well, when we take in a breath the diaphragm, which is the large muscle between the lungs and the stomach, moves down and what you will feel will be the stomach muscles which are connected to that. So already you are connecting to your breath.

Let's look at the diaphragm in more detail. The diaphragm is a dome-shaped muscle located below our lungs. It separates the heart and lungs from the digestive organs. It works like bellows, taking air down and then pushing it out. This works without any conscious effort on our part. However, it is useful to learn how to be aware of controlling this muscle. You may need to be more aware of your diaphragm when nervous or when you need more volume. By consciously inflating the diaphragm more fully, you will arrest the shallow breathing of 'fight or flight' and you can also hugely increase the amount of air moving in and out of the lungs to enable you to increase volume without straining your vocal chords, which is what most people do when trying to increase volume.

When you take a breath the ribcage opens and the diaphragm moves down. The rib cage and abdominal muscles are now open and you should feel wider. I liken it to the opening of a squeezebox that has a horizontal movement not a vertical movement. This is a useful image as it takes you away from lifting your shoulders if that is what you are prone to do. You should feel that your waist is expanding not your upper chest.

We have 12 pairs of ribs. The ones that concern us are the lower ones, the 11th and 12th ones. These are only attached to the spine at the back but are free at the front earning them the name 'floating ribs'. The top ribs have more limited movement but these floating ribs allow for further expansion of the lungs. So really opening the lower ribs and allowing the diaphragm to fully descend can allow the breath to be filled lower in the body.

Breathing

What happens when you take in a breath?

The following is a very brief physiological description. You don't need to know this to breathe properly, and you can skip it if you like, but a knowledge of how sound is created will help you understand the critical role of proper breathing.

When you breathe in, or inhale, your diaphragm contracts and moves downward. This increases the space in your chest cavity, into which your lungs expand. The intercostal muscles between your ribs also help enlarge the chest cavity. They contract to pull your rib cage both upward and outward when you inhale.

As your lungs expand, air is sucked in through your nose or mouth. The air travels down your windpipe and into your lungs. After passing through your bronchial tubes, the air finally reaches and enters the alveoli (air sacs).

Through the very thin walls of the alveoli, oxygen from the air passes to the surrounding capillaries. At the same time, carbon dioxide moves from the capillaries into the air sacs.

Oxygen-rich blood from the lungs is carried through a network of capillaries to the pulmonary vein. This vein delivers the oxygen-rich blood to the left side of the heart. The left side of the heart pumps the blood to the rest of the body. There, the oxygen in the blood moves from blood vessels into surrounding tissues.

What happens when you breathe out?

When you breathe out, or exhale, your diaphragm relaxes and moves upward into the chest cavity. The intercostal muscles between the ribs also relax to reduce the space in the chest cavity.

As the space in the chest cavity gets smaller, air rich in carbon dioxide is forced out of your lungs and windpipe, and then out of your nose or mouth.

It is this breath, this column of air, that passes over the vocal chords causing them to vibrate and make sound. This sound is then reinforced or amplified with the help of the face, head, chest, throat and nose. Further amplification comes from the room in which you are speaking.

Breathing

How to use breathing to control 'Fight or Flight'

When you are experiencing 'Fight or Flight', one of the physiological symptoms is shallow breathing. It boosts athletic activity but is not helpful in public speaking. Getting control over your breathing is really the best way to rid yourself of any physical and mental symptoms that are detrimental to standing up and sounding assured and calm.

Returning to the diaphragm, this is the muscle which will give you control over shallow breathing. It is this shallow breathing which is reminding the brain that there is a threat, so it makes sense to change that message to the brain.

I would suggest that you try out any of the following breathing exercises while at home and in a calm environment until you really understand the connection between deeper breathing and feeling calmer. Then when you are in court and feeling anxious, you will be able to control your shallow breathing more easily as the connection will already have been made. It's always advisable to make sure that you are physically relaxed first before working on your breathing.

The first thing to check out is whether you are breathing in the upper chest or in the belly. Below are 3 ways of checking how you breathe.

1. Stand in front of a mirror. Take in a very deep breath while watching your chest. If you notice that your chest rises along with your shoulders, and your stomach has been sucked in, then you are only breathing with the top part of the lungs, which means that you are breathing incorrectly.

2. **QR** Lie on the floor with your head supported and with your knees bent. Place a heavy book on your midriff and breathe deeply. You might be able to check whether your belly is moving with the help of the weight pressing down and by actually seeing the book rise and fall. If this isn't happening then in all probability you are breathing shallowly in the upper chest.

3. Stand in front of a long mirror and place your hands on either side of your waist with your fingers spread and pointing towards the waist. As you take deep breaths in and out you should see the gap change in size between your

hands. As you breathe in the gap should widen and as you breathe out your hands will move closer together. Press quite firmly as you do this and you should also *feel* the lateral and forward expansion.

These exercises will have shown you how you breathe while relaxed or at rest. They may have shown you that you breathe using the upper chest or in fact you may be breathing effectively. However, in times of stress this may change. The 'fight or flight' response may indeed be subtle, a holding in of the stomach muscles for example, but that is still a form of holding your breath. Upper chest breathing then would have to come into play at this point bringing with it an underlying feeling of discomfort or stress.

Even if you feel that you are breathing the way nature intended, it would still be worth trying out the following three exercises. When we move on to looking at how to support speech these basic exercises will be useful.

1. Physical Connection A
Put your hands on your ribs as in the above exercise no. 3. Breathe out – blow out until you can't blow anymore. Wait a second or two until your body insists you take in a breath. Allow the breath in and you will experience the sudden flow of air. You will feel the ribs to the front and side expanding. This is often quite a powerful feeling. Repeat this a few times. You may be surprised by how physical this feeling is, reminding yourself possibly of how rarely you take a full breath. Don't concern yourself with *thinking* of breathing in, as this will happen automatically.

Another way of developing an awareness of the breath reaching low into the lungs is to try the following exercise.

2. Physical Connection B
Sit back to front on a simple chair with a back and rest your arms on the back with your legs akimbo either side of the chair. Lean forward. Rest your arms on the chair back. Just start breathing naturally but with each breath focus on the lower back area. You will gradually become more aware of these floating ribs moving in and out.

When you feel confident that you are breathing more fully, sit normally on an office chair and check that you still have the connection to a lower fuller breath.

Breathing

Use this key exercise to cope with 'Fight or Flight'.

3. The Flower and the Candle QR

Sit comfortably on a simple chair, making sure your feet are planted firmly. Imagine that in one hand you are holding a flower with a wonderful rich scent and in the other hand you are holding a lit candle. Bring the hand with the flower up to just below your nose and breathe in the scent of your flower through your nose, imagining the scent going all the way down to your diaphragm. Then blow out calmly and steadily through your mouth towards your candle in the other hand. This out breath should be steady. You want to picture making the flame flicker. You don't want to blow it out with a sudden puff of breath. It is this steady out breath which will help you to feel calm. Once you feel you understand how this works you can place your hands loosely on your lap and just imagine the flower and candle in front of you.

The beauty of this exercise is that you can do it in court while waiting to speak and no one will know you're doing it.

Don't rush any of the above exercises. Sometimes it takes a while to make that connection.

Now that you have managed to recognise the shallow upper chest breathing, symptomatic of anxiety, and can consciously bring the breath down, you are in control of your breathing.

It's useful to check your breathing from time to time. You will be surprised at how often you may literally be holding your breath. The threat of embarrassment, of being misunderstood, of looking foolish or of mild stress can cause the body to think that it is under threat. We respond to these 'threats' exactly as if our lives were at stake. Given how often, especially in the early days of our careers, that we may experience these feelings it is then unsurprising that our breathing becomes arrested in the upper chest.

Whenever you feel any anxiety, simply breathe making sure that the breath is deep and wide. Concentrate on a slow outward breath and the in-breath will take care of itself. Allow yourself the time to breathe fully.

How to use breath to support the voice

It may seem unnecessary to learn how to breathe properly but breath is one of the few bodily functions that we can do both automatically and voluntarily. So, specifically when speaking in public, where a quick intake and slow release of breath is required, understanding how to control one's breath is vital.

Physically we all vary in size and shape and our voices reflect these differences but we all have control over how we use the breath and that can make all the difference between a voice which is easy to listen to and one that isn't.

If you do not have enough breath, your voice may not reach the listeners. Too much breath and your voice may sound pushy with aggressive consonants, or simply be too loud.

The two key areas here are: taking in the right amount of breath required for speech; and learning how to release it in a controlled way.

Most lawyers, on seeing the size of a court at the start of their career, worry that they will not be heard. Taking in the right amount of breath will help to produce a bigger sound but not if it is coupled with anxiety.

If you start to push your voice because of tension, the following things may happen:

- Your voice will sound higher pitched and tight
- Your voice will be restricted to the upper body and cut out the lower tones, sounding thin and mean
- Your listeners will be aware of the sound rather than the words
- Your energy will be coming from the throat leading to vocal problems in the future

I cannot say often enough: check your posture and eliminate excess tension before working on breath and the voice.

In order for your voice to sound warm and rich, you want to engage the breathing mechanisms at the base of the ribs. This way the whole body becomes involved. If your breathing is limited to the upper chest, your voice will reflect that. We've all

Breathing

heard people who get by with very little breath but their voices lack physical and emotional depth.

This first exercise is to help you connect to your diaphragm.

- Lie on the floor with your head supported on a large book, legs bent and feet flat on the floor. Spread your back as much as possible.
- Imagine your neck and spine lengthening.
- Put the backs of your hands /knuckles on the bottom of the rib cage.
- Breathe in through the nose, feeling the ribs move out under your hands.
- Sigh out through an open mouth. Let *all* the air out to the last drop. Now follow your body as it will tell you when it needs to take in the next breath. Again, you will be aware of the ribs opening around the back and sides.
- Do this two or three more times, breathing in through the nose and out through the mouth. Use the body's natural energy and rhythm. Allow the body to direct when you should take the next breath. Often we breathe in before the body is ready, we snatch at the breath and then we breathe out before we've finished breathing in.
- Now try this standing up.

By now you should be becoming aware of breathing deeper in your body. Try not to let the upper part of the chest move.

If you're not too lightheaded at this point, move on to the next part of the exercise. This will introduce you to connecting breathing to speaking.

QR Breathing

- Breathe in through the nose and out through the mouth until a smooth and relaxed rhythm has settled.
- Then begin a mental count of inspiration and expiration. Count in for 3 and out for 3.
- Once you've got used to this, you can start to vary the count. Try aiming for a shorter count for the in-breath and a longer count for the out-breath. A count of 2 for inspiration and 4 for expiration is good to begin with.

Breathing

- Check that the intercostal muscles are controlling the outgoing sigh, as this is the whole point of this exercise.
- Wait before you breathe in again so you can actually feel the impulse to take the next breath.
- As you start to become more comfortable with this exercise you could decrease the inspiration count and extend the expiration time. This now mirrors the pattern of breathing necessary for speech.
- Finally, repeat this exercise but vocalise the counting, starting at a low number and increasing to match your breath capacity.
- Finally, replace the external counting with some nursery rhymes so that you are relating connected speech to the outbreath.

By now you should be more aware of opening up the ribs and controlling the out-breath.

At all times try to keep the relaxation and stay connected to your centre.

The following exercise is useful in that it shows you how important breath control and focus is when speaking in different sized areas. We need much less breath control when speaking to someone standing beside us, but firmer breath control when filling a bigger space.

- Stand in a room and choose 5 points at varying distances.
- Use the breath to connect with these points.
- Take in a breath through the mouth and send the breath out to where your chosen point is.
- Don't allow the head and neck to stick forward. Allow the breath to come from your centre. Stay relaxed. It's a game!
- Be aware of how much pressure and control is needed for each point.
- Take time to allow the breath to reach the further points.
- The final step is to introduce voice but make sure it is supported by the breath. Again, choose the points to which you want the voice to travel but replace the sigh with your Nursery Rhyme.
- Can you feel the difference from near to far points?

Breathing

Caution – if you are not used to breathing fully, you may feel light-headed so don't over-do these breathing exercises initially. However, what you are working towards is increasing breath capacity so that in court, or when public speaking, every word can be heard even those at the very end of the sentence. In court especially, the last word may be the most important.

17 POSTURE

"I sometimes feel as if I'm about to fall over so I clutch the lectern to steady myself."

I know that most people who attend my training courses expect to launch into voice work. They have some vague ideas that they may be working on old-fashioned elocution exercises and will sound more 'posh'. I have to explain to them that there are basic issues which need to be looked at first before working on speech. In most professional voice books we firstly look at relaxation, breathing and posture before tackling voice work. So try to eliminate tension before looking at your posture.

In this chapter I'll be looking at:

- Why posture is important
- What good posture is
- How to achieve good posture

Why posture is important?

We've all heard that where the mind leads, the body will follow. This is an important realisation: that by changing what you believe, you can actually change what your body is capable of doing. But it's critical to understand that the body leads the mind, too. Stand up straight, walk tall, and you will actually think and feel better. You will also conserve energy as muscles are the biggest energy consumers in the body and poor posture means they have to work overtime, depleting energy. Your posture can in fact seriously affect your mood and attitude to the situation you are in. It not only affects how you feel but will affect those watching. From the moment you walk into the court, or indeed from the moment you are seen strolling around and chatting outside the courtroom, you are transmitting an attitude. This may be an attitude which you have chosen to reflect, but most of us carry with us attitudes and feelings of which we are unaware but with which we have grown comfortable. It is these habitual patterns that usually need attention.

We also need to look at posture in relation to the voice, as mentioned above. The reason is that if you keep the centre of gravity low, you are freeing the back and abdominal muscles so that they can be used more effectively in supporting the breath rather than in maintaining balance. So if you are someone who habitually stands with your feet together and knees straight, you are shifting the centre of gravity upwards so the back and abdominal muscles are required to help maintain balance rather than support voice production.

Why do we walk or stand the way we do? Well, let's go back a bit, to childhood in fact. When we were young children, we were more likely to have the posture which we were designed to have. We were more balanced, centred and comfortable in this position. We sat, squatted, lifted, walked and ran in perfect alignment. Our speech reflected our free bodies too, with energised relaxed voices. However, as the years went on, life changed us. But because this happened gradually we were unaware that we were changing from how nature intended us to be, until one day we realised that our jaws were jutting out, our shoulders were hunched or our weight rested predominantly on one foot. We have now acquired distorted and misshapen ways of holding ourselves. We slouch, slump, shuffle and laze awkwardly and inefficiently upon our frame. We become defensive if criticised, saying "but this is me".

Why did this happen? I put most of the blame on adolescence. Look at teenagers and check out their physicality. Many of them stand with very low energy (it looks cooler), sagging in the middle, with rounded shoulders and eyes cast down and so forth. If you think for a moment about teenagers' speech, it reflects their posture, with a lack of connection and presence, as witnessed by the mumbling and tailing away at the end of sentences. The vocal and physical attitudes of adolescents reflect their attitude or fashion but also their insecurities.

Most of us, as we leave this stage of our lives behind, improve on the worst of the adolescent habits but, as they seemed to serve us well for many years, we are often unconscious of some of them and still carry the memory of them around. And that is certainly true when faced with a challenge which we don't feel up to, as in those first nervous appearances in a courtroom.

Thus it is not uncommon for me to see young lawyers quite unconsciously betraying their discomfort and anxiety. They may want to portray confidence and gravitas but their posture and body language scream a different set of messages.

Then, on top of adolescence, we continue to work on our bad posture by the very nature of our lives. How heavy is the shoulder bag or briefcase that you have carried around for years? What about your favourite office chair which is tilting your spine back? You may also subconsciously imitate close family and friends in the way they gesture or stand. There is no doubt though that a lack of physical activity, combined with too many hours in front of a computer, can bring about long-term damage to our bodies.

So there are three main reasons for working on and being aware of your posture:

1. What your posture says about you.
2. How you feel about yourself
3. Your voice

What good posture is

Good posture is not the old-fashioned army stance, with shoulders held tightly back and stomach sucked in. Rather, it is about the natural alignment of the head, neck and torso. Good posture involves keeping your body in alignment and maintaining the natural curve of the spine while sitting or standing. If this can be achieved it should bring about a sense of ease. The message which a court practitioner would want to transmit would be relaxed competence, and this starts with the correct posture.

How to check what your posture is like? Look in a mirror, ideally from the side or get a friend to take a few photos of you from different angles in your normal state. The other clues to help you will be checking where you hold tension or get aches and pains. If, after appearing in court, you feel that your thighs are sore then that's a giveaway as to where you hold tension. If you suffer from frequent headaches you may have neck or shoulder tightness. Get used to reading your body. Pay attention to what it's telling you. Be prepared to accept that, as you start to work on your posture, it may feel awkward. That is only natural if you are changing something which you have adapted to for years.

Posture

The areas to check

Feet
What we are working towards is a feeling of balance, so I like to start with the feet. Check that they are shoulder-width apart and parallel. If one foot is always forward of the other, this means that further up the line, one hip is further forward than the other. The body should rest lightly on both heels and soles. Really feel the connection to the floor, as it will help make you feel grounded. Many people stand with their weight resting on one foot. This is adding to the 'fight or flight' message to the brain, as you are literally poised for flight. Imagine that there are roots growing down from your feet supporting you. I don't want you to feel that you are rooted to the spot. Quite the contrary: I want you to feel that your feet are supporting you in an easy, balanced manner but you are in a state of readiness. This is not a passive position, just easy.

Legs
If you feel your legs are shaking when you stand up to speak, it's possible that you are tensing and locking them. If you feel that you are locking the thighs or knees, you will be affecting the spine and lower back. Try shaking out your legs before going into court to remind yourself that that is an area on which you need to keep an eye. Mentally say to yourself when you stand up "Soft knees" and remind yourself of that from time to time, as tension has a habit of creeping back in. Your thighs should be facing forward and loose. Your calf muscles should also be loose.

The Spine
The way you lie, sit, stand, walk and run is affected by the spine. It transmits to the audience messages such as you are tense or relaxed, tired or rested, old or young and so forth and it helps to transform the shape of your body and the sound of the voice. The spine influences the tuning of the whole body and if it is held stiffly, coordination is disturbed. When you work on exercises for the spine which involve rolling and unrolling, always lower the head first on the downward movement. If you suffer from anxiety in the courtroom, this may involve you holding tension in the muscles in the back and this can alter your breathing pattern, affecting your ability to control the voice. If you feel that your voice is soft or shaky, the root of the problem may well be the spine.

Posture

The Stomach

How many of us suck in our tummies when we stand up to speak? I'm afraid that if you are speaking in public, then it's the worst thing to do as you are actually constricting the breath, so the only advice is to let it all hang out. Try some of the breathing exercises in this book to remind yourself to 'let go'.

Pelvis

This is probably the most important part of your body to be aware of. If your pelvis is leaning too far forward, the body has to compensate to remain upright. If the pelvis is tilted too far back, the body sags backward and the shoulders and head move forward to compensate. If your pelvis is twisted to one side (one hip higher than the other), the whole body strains to compensate for this misalignment.

Shoulders

So many people work at computers now that most of us have some problems here. The shoulders are so close to the neck that problems in one area tend to affect the other. The shoulders should be on the same plane when seen from the front. Look closely. You may have one shoulder placed slightly higher than the other – it might be the side you favour for carrying things – shopping, handbags and children. Check that they are not raised through tension or rounded from habitual leaning over a desk. Try raising the shoulders and saying to yourself 'Let go' and then dropping them. Don't reposition them or you will simply replace the tension.

Neck

A good mantra would be "keep the neck free". If there is tension in the neck, the voice will be strained and will feel trapped in the throat. Try and keep the front of the neck loose.

Head

The head weighs more than we realise so if it is balanced incorrectly on the spine that will adversely affect the voice, again due to misalignment. The head should rest balanced squarely on top of the spine. Try and picture the crown of the head as being the highest part of your body. If your head is in a forward position, then this causes strain in the back of your neck and is a common cause of headaches. Your chin should be level – not raised, pulled down or jutting forward.

Posture

How to achieve good posture

If you have checked out all the parts of the body listed above, you will now be ready to try out some of these simple exercises which will help you to achieve good posture.

Posture stretch A
Reach your arms out in front of you, link your fingers and push your palms away.

Reach up to the sky, link your fingers and push your palms away, keeping your shoulders down. This will stretch your back and spine.

Posture stretch B
Lie on your back on the floor with your knees bent, feet on the floor, arms out to the side and your palms facing down.

Gently drop your knees to the right, but keep your left shoulder blade on the floor.

Turn you head to the left and relax into the stretch.
Repeat on the other side.

Simple alignment exercise QR

Start by standing with your feet shoulder-width apart, shoulders dropped and relaxed, back wide and head balanced.
Hug yourself with arms criss-crossed and reaching for the shoulder blades, but tenderly, not with a rough grip. Keep the shoulders released in this hold: neither tense nor bunch them. Keep your feet apart beneath the hips and parallel with one another.

Bend the knees gradually and, still hugging yourself, flop over from the waist. Breathe in deeply. You should feel the back open.

Still in this position take several unhurried breaths. Let the arms drop down. To resume the standing posture, straighten the knees and slowly reassemble a

Posture

straightened back, slowly coming up through the spine, vertebra by vertebra. Once again, do not place the shoulders but let them find their natural position.

As you come up, be aware not to hoist yourself into place by lifting the upper chest. If this happens, place your hand there to still it.

Stand centred and open your arms out in a welcoming embrace. Feel the energy flow through your arms. In this position, drop the shoulders. Then allow the arms to return to your side. The upper chest should feel very open and there should be a sensation of breath going into the back.

From this natural standing position, move steadily up on to the balls of your feet by applying a steady, even flow of energy so that you rise slowly. Then slowly lower your heels until your feet are firmly on the ground. The more you do this, the more natural it will feel.

> *Note: If you had to shift your weight around to compensate for feeling off balance it may tell you one of two things: if you had to shift your weight forward to rise, it may mean that you lean back with too much weight on your heels; conversely, if you had to shift your weight back, you may habitually have too much weight on the front of your toes.*

How does this make you feel? After trying any exercise out it is useful to pay attention to how the body feels. You might want to ask yourself whether you feel more energised, purposeful or lighter?

Some people query this kind of work with me. They may point out that it feels and looks unnatural or they look bland. These are valid points. To answer the issue of the new stance looking and feeling unnatural – this is quite common when the body is readjusting from the habitual patterns of so many years. It will feel awkward, but all I would say is that you should give it time and see how you feel after a few weeks.

As to the point that one looks 'bland', I'd prefer to replace the word 'bland' with 'neutral'. This is a useful word in any actor's lexicon. It's a way of getting rid of a performer's own tics and mannerisms which may be quite inappropriate to the role he or she is playing. I would suggest that in the role of a court practitioner, sometimes your own personality can be sending out the wrong signals and working against you.

Posture

Rather, think of this new stance as one helping you achieve a state of readiness, with the idea that any movement or action could begin from this. This is not a bland or passive state but a position of vitality. Add to this position of balance your eye line and you may feel more ready for action. Your eyes should look towards a point in the distance. This stance will help you to feel anticipation, rather like the tennis player crouching forward, ready to move in any direction, or like a runner about to start a race.

By replacing the word 'bland' with 'neutral' you are stripping away mannerisms and habits which form your outward personality, leaving you unencumbered by attitude and traits.

I have mentioned eyeline. If it has been pointed out to you that you look downwards or if you feel that maintaining eye contact is a challenge, you might want to try out this actor's exercise. Your posture will be helped by facing the world not the floor.

Eyeline exercise QR

Check your posture first.
Place your eyes at a specific point at the other side of the room.
Keep your eyes on this point and walk towards it. Don't look away.
When you arrive at this point, stop, let your eyes choose another spot and then turn in that direction.
Walk towards the new point.
Keep walking to new fixed points.

Being able to look across the room and maintain a level eyeline adds to the posture which you have been working on to create a total image. You will be transmitting a positive image before you have even opened your mouth. From the moment you enter the courthouse, bear this in mind. You will look purposeful and focussed. You will also feel purposeful and focussed.

Posture

How to walk correctly 1 QR

Keep your back straight, knees soft and buttocks squeezed. Imagine a string in the middle of the head pulling your head up. Then imagine someone pulling on the string, which in turn leads you to start walking.

How to walk correctly 2 QR

Another trick is to lean against a wall, letting it support you, get balanced and then focus on your forehead. Then set off to walk allowing the forehead to lead.

Posture while sitting

Lawyers spend a lot of time sitting in court. Good posture doesn't just refer to a standing position but to the right way to sit. You are as capable of sending out the wrong message while sitting as standing. Your habitual sitting position may be slightly slumped which could transmit to the jury that you are defeated or too tired to fight the case.

> Sit up with your back straight. Your buttocks should touch the back of the chair.
> Distribute your body weight evenly on both hips.
> Bend your knees at a right angle.
> Don't cross your legs.
> Keep your feet flat on the floor.
> Keep your shoulders relaxed. Rest your arms on the chair or table.
> Try to avoid sitting in the same position for more than 30 minutes.
> Try not to twist your body when looking around. Instead turn your whole body.

The transition from sitting to standing will be smoother as well since you are sitting in a position of readiness. The easiest way to rise is to move to the front of the seat, then stand up by straightening your legs. Avoid bending forward at your waist.

Posture

Given that there are so many benefits to correcting your posture, it would make sense to be more mindful of how you sit and stand. Below are some more suggestions.

- Spend ten minutes each morning doing some simple stretches. This is particularly important if you have a fairly sedentary job.
- Take a few moments each day to focus on your posture, e.g. when you are checking yourself in the mirror before leaving the house.
- Mentally work your way down your body, straightening up your spine, bringing your shoulders down away from your ears and pulling in your stomach muscles.
- Spend a few minutes laid out flat on the floor, with no cushions or support. Do this at least once a day.
- Try to avoid relying on the back of your chair for support. Come forward in your seat, keeping a small curve in your lower back. This will help to prevent the pain caused when you hunch over your computer.
- Don't cross your legs when sitting because it over-stretches one side of your legs, slowly misaligning the pelvis and spine.
- Only carry essential items. Carrying large heavy bags on one shoulder puts unequal pressure on the spine. Opt for a small bag and regularly swap the shoulder you carry it on. Alternatively, use a backpack that sits on both shoulders.

Footwear
Ronnie has already spoken about dress in his opening chapter. I'd like to add the problem of what wearing high-heeled shoes can do to your posture. I know that many women feel more confident wearing high-heeled shoes, especially if you want to look taller but they really don't help your posture or balance.

When you wear high heels your foot slides forward, putting pressure on your toes and redistributing your weight incorrectly. Your body tilts forward. Instinctively you then try to compensate by arching your back, putting strain on knees and lower back.

The long-term damage to your body is considerable but short term you quite simply don't feel grounded and supported. If you really feel you can't give up the 2 inch stilettos can I suggest you try a lower chunkier heel as this will spread the load more evenly. Your feet are your base of support. If they aren't happy, nothing above them will be.

It would also be a good idea to consider the following if you really want to avoid a lifetime of back pain and tension headaches.

> *Pilates* can strengthen the body's own muscular 'corset' that supports and protects the body during everyday movements. This corset of muscles around the torso often becomes weak after years of poor posture.

> *Yoga* releases tension and restores flexibility to muscles and joints. Yoga's poses and breathing exercises can address many aspects of poor posture, from rounded shoulders to muscular imbalances. Iyengar yoga, with its focus on technique and precision, is particularly good for posture.

> *Alexander technique* re-teaches everyday movements such as walking and getting up from a chair to consciously change your bad posture habits.

> *Feldenkrais* teaches awareness of movement through gentle prompting and guided touch. This helps the body to move more fluidly. Flexibility is thought to improve after just one session.

18 VOICE

"The Sheriff interrupted me to complain that I was going too fast."

The voice is as much a part of the job description as legal knowledge.

In this chapter I'll be looking at:

- Why the voice is important in court work
- How to work on making your speech clearer
- How to create vocal energy
- How to speak at the right pace
- How to add variety to your delivery

Why the voice is important in court work

At the very least you should be audible. You should never speak so fast that the sheriff has to ask you to slow down. Your accent should not impede people's ability to understand you and you should be able to keep the interest of those who have to listen to you. That list is actually quite challenging but the good news is that with some regular practice, following some of my exercises, you really can achieve these basic courtroom vocal skills.

But why is working on the voice so challenging? I think it's because the voice is very personal to each of us. Our voice reflects who we are in the most intimate way and carries with it our history, both physical and psychological. It tells the listener where we come from and reflects our class, attitudes, mannerisms and self-esteem. Instinctively we know this and we are afraid that when we open our mouths to speak in court we may be revealing who we are and what we might be lacking.

Voice

I am saddened by how many people don't like the sound of their own voice. If you are one of these people it's possible that the quality of your voice will reflect this attitude and that in itself will be causing you problems. That lack of commitment to speech will prevent you having a strong, flexible, professional court voice. However, using the voice is a physical action and if you are prepared to work on the muscles that make speech, you will see a change. This may require you to be bolder in your approach to using your voice but the rewards are great. The more efficient is the voice, the more accurate will be the message you wish to convey.

Reminder

Let me emphasise though that the voice will not work to its optimum capability until you have addressed the contents of my previous chapters. So check out that you are not holding unnecessary tension, that your posture is balanced and that you are breathing from the diaphragm.

How to work on making your speech clearer

Speech is made up of words. Words are made up of consonants and vowels. (The consonants are b c d f g h j k l m n p q r s t v w x y z, ch and th and the vowels are a e i o u.) You need them both and they fulfil different roles. The vowels add energy and emotion and the consonants add commitment and precision and carry the intelligence of the sentence. Vowels add colour and consonants add clarity. However, there needs to be a delicate balance between vowels and consonants. If the vowels dominate, the sense may be drowned by too much feeling. If the consonants dominate, you might marvel at the clarity of the speech but remain unmoved.

If you don't take the time to really shape these vowels and consonants your speech will lack life and energy, you will be harder to listen to and you will sound bland. In normal day-to-day conversation you can get away with this but put yourself in the courtroom where the job demands that you fill the space and your voice will not be up to the task. More is required. It is not the listeners' job to try to work out what you are saying. Most people are courteous and will try to follow what a dull speaker is saying but only up to a point and in the end will just tune out. Lazy speech indicates a lack of commitment and can be taken two ways, both negative: you don't care or you can't be bothered.

Voice

So the first and simplest way to achieve clear speech is to work on shaping and committing to these vowels and consonants.

Lack of clarity often comes from tension in the speech articulators (jaw, lips and tongue). It's worth warming up those areas before trying out vocal exercises.

Pre-vocal warm-up QR

Begin by screwing up your face as tight as you can. Hold for a few seconds and then let go. Repeat.

Imagine you are holding something under your nose which has a revolting smell and wrinkle up your face in an exaggerated fashion, then let go.

Now imagine that you are suddenly surprised – stretch open your mouth and eyes for a couple of seconds and then let go.

Imagine that your face is made of putty.

Make gentle fists, place them against your cheeks and gently draw them down, imagining that you are stretching the jaw as the putty is pulled down. Repeat. You should feel that your jaw is less tight after this exercise.

Imagine that you have a chocolate-covered toffee in your mouth. Chew it round and round in a relaxed but exaggerated manner. Then use your tongue to lick off the chocolate that has smeared on to your lips.

Now imagine that you are a cat lapping up milk.

Then blow your lips out as if you were a horse snorting. Repeat.

Now make some energetic air kisses adding the accompanying sound 'Mwaah'.

Finally, yawn while counting out 1, 2, 3. This should help to open up the throat.

Vocal exercises

These exercises will help you exercise the speech muscles. They should be done regularly to counteract lazy speech. Try them out. You won't want to use them all but there may be one or two which you feel help you the most.

Voice

The following is a useful exercise to help you realise how much physical activity is required to really shape these vowels and consonants.

The Cork exercise QR

Have ready an extract from a piece of legal work. Read it out loud.
(You could use the extract that follows, which is the one you can see if accessing this QR code.)

> "Consider this unfortunate woman's act as though you yourself had each committed it. Every living being is capable of attack, if sufficiently provoked. Assault lies dormant within us all. It requires only circumstances to set it in violent motion. I ask you for a verdict of not guilty. There was no murder attempt here, only a pathetic attempt to save a home."
>
> *Adam's Rib* (1949 American film written by Ruth Gordon and Garson Kanin and directed by George Cukor.)

Then take a cork and place it in your mouth horizontally holding it in place between your teeth. Don't grip too hard – just enough pressure to keep it in place near the front of your mouth.

Now read out loud a couple of times the paragraph from your document, speaking very slowly and shaping every syllable of each word in an exaggerated manner.

Now remove the cork, read the passage again and see if you can feel and hear the difference. You may note that you are working harder to shape the words and that the sound will be fuller and easier to listen to.

Voice

The Vowels exercise QR

Take a short extract from a newspaper or a legal document. Read out a few of the sentences pronouncing the vowels only (A, E, I, O, U). They need to be pronounced the way they would be if spoken. You might find it helpful initially to pronounce a word fully to hear it, then repeat it again but omitting the consonants. It's also helpful to mark where the consonants would be by leaving a small pause so there is a distinction between the different vowel sounds. It's tricky and you will sound strange but persevere because the rewards are worth it. Every few phrases try comparing your delivery by alternating between including and omitting the consonants. As in the cork exercise, you should start to hear fuller vowels.

Helping the deaf

Imagine reading to someone who is hard of hearing or even totally deaf. Shouting does not help but exaggerated formation of speech and more facial animation does. Generally more vocal and facial energy is needed.

Try this out with a partner. Stand at a distance and use a stage whisper to communicate. See how much they can pick up as they will in effect be lip-reading.

Tongue twisters

The following tongue twisters include all the sounds used in speech. Don't rush through them. Say them quite deliberately and slowly. The aim of this is to help your brain recognise how much work is required to shape the vowels and consonants. Really savour the sounds and picture every sound leaving your mouth. Don't throw away the little words like in, of, at, it, as, and so on – they give sense to the rest of the sentence and are as important. So shape every word to the same value.

> Roberta ran rings around the Roman ruins.
>
> Picky people pick Peter Pan peanut butter, 'tis the peanut butter picky people pick.
>
> I scream, you scream, we all scream for ice cream!
>
> How many cans can a cannibal nibble if a cannibal can nibble cans?

Four furious friends fought for the phone.

Green glass globes glow greenly.

The great Greek grape growers grow great Greek grapes.

Bobby Bippy bought a bat
Bobby Bippy bought a ball
With his bat Bob banged the ball
Banged it bump against the wall.

Peggy Babcock, Peggy Babcock, Peggy Babcock.

Two tiny tigers take two taxis to town.

Double bubble gum, bubbles double.

The sixth sick sheik's sixth sheep is sick.

A fuller warm up

The following piece is useful for continuing awareness of consonants. Again really shape all the sounds, being particularly aware of the ends of words.

The Song of the Sock (Dr Seuss)
Give me the gift of a grip-top sock,
A clip-drape, ship-shape, tip-top sock,
Not a spiv-slick, slap-stick, slip-shod stock,
But a plastic, elastic, slack swap-slop
From a slapdash, flash, cash-haberdash shop;

Not a knick-knack, knit-lock,
Knock-kneed, knickerbocker sock
With a mock-shot, blot-mottled
Trick, tick-tocker clock;
Not a rucked-up, puckered-up, flop-top sock
Nor a super-sheer seersucker
Pukka sack-smock sock;

Not a spot-speckled, frog-freckled
Cheap Sheik's sock
Off a hotch-potch, moss-blotch
Botched Scotch block;
Nothing slip-slop, drip-drop
Flip-flop or clip-clop:
Tip me to a tip-top
Grip-top
Sock.

The following speech is useful for further awareness of vowels. Again, for the purposes of working on your voice, exaggerate all the vowels in this speech. Try and work in the biggest room available and really fill the space with these vowels, sending them out to the furthest point.

'Tomorrow, and Tomorrow, and Tomorrow'
Tomorrow, and tomorrow, and tomorrow,
Creeps in this petty pace from day to day,
To the last syllable of recorded time;
And all our yesterdays have lighted fools
The way to dusty death. Out, out, brief candle!
Life's but a walking shadow, a poor player
That struts and frets his hour upon the stage,
And then is heard no more. It is a tale
Told by an idiot, full of sound and fury,
Signifying nothing.

Macbeth (William Shakespeare)

So now you are fully warmed up. However, it's worth mentioning here that, although physically warming up the speech organs is helpful, there are also other reasons why speech can be indistinct, or why you may trail off at the end of sentences.

It may be that you are not fully committed to your argument and your voice will reflect this uncertainty. It's worth taking a pause before speaking to formulate exactly what you want to say. The voice can only reflect what information the brain is passing to it. If you are not thinking right through to the end of the thought, that can be an explanation of why you appear to run out of vocal energy.

Voice

Putting it all together

At this stage you can now start reading anything out loud, 5 minutes every day to remind yourself of what clear speech is: newspaper articles of different moods, extracts from Charles Dickens, legal papers, poetry and prose. I am including two film courtroom speeches and you might want to play around with them, focussing on the vowels and consonants. See what happens when you really attack the consonants, for example on the words 'strike' 'verdict' and 'pathetic'; and the reverse, when you savour the vowels where you might want to draw attention to an emotional or heightened moment.

> "Consider this unfortunate woman's act as though you yourselves had each committed it. Every living being is capable of attack, if sufficiently provoked. Assault lies dormant within us all. It requires only circumstance to set it in violent motion. I ask you for a verdict of not guilty. There was no murder attempt here, only a pathetic attempt to save a home."
>
> *Adam's Rib*, Katherine Hepburn

> "This great nation has long been a great commercial power. Now it seems there exists a growing compulsion to use that power merely to beget more power. Money merely to beget more money, irrespective of the true cost to the nation's soul. And it is this sickness, a kind of moral blindness, commerce without conscience, which threatens to strike at the very soul of this nation. And the only remedy that I can see is to strike back and to strike now!"
>
> Sir Robert Chiltern, Address to Parliament on the Proposed Canal Project in *An Ideal Husband*.

The benefits of fully shaping consonants and vowels are numerous.

Sloppy speech confuses your listeners in court. For example, you intend to say the word 'isn't', but due to poor articulation the listeners only hear 'is' which is quite different. The same with 'did' and 'didn't'.

Sharper speech not only allows you to sound more confident but also helps you to feel more confident. If you are a nervous speaker there's nothing more guaranteed to make you even more anxious than to hear yourself stumble over words. Hearing yourself sound confident from the moment you stand up to speak will help you overcome stage fright more quickly.

Another plus to clear enunciation is that if you generally have a soft voice, shaping vowels and consonants will make your voice sound stronger.

If you are concerned about your accent, taking care to speak clearly will help enormously. Accents are acceptable, unclear speech isn't.

How to create vocal Energy

It takes mental and physical energy to communicate fully. We all recognise those speakers who have not grasped that they need to do the work so that the listener only has to follow the message. We've looked at how important the breath is in supporting the voice, at how important it is to rid ourselves of excess tension and how much work is involved in really shaping the words. Underpinning all this has to be the right level of energy.

How do we create that? A physical and vocal warm-up will certainly get you part of the way there but it's also about an awareness of how your voice can sound when you are relaxed and really wanting to communicate.

Think of times in your life when you feel your voice had more life and energy: were you socialising with friends, or on the sports field, or at a bar trying to be heard over music?

The common factor is that you will have been relaxed and have had a need to communicate. Think of how you found a voice across a games field and how you were able, even while running, to call out to another player.

Try out some of these exercises to remind your brain of how free your voice can sound especially when linked with physical activity. I'm not suggesting that you move physically in court – the memory of what your voice can sound like is what we're working towards. With experience you will then be able to re-create this free voice by just imagining it.

Try out the following exercises at home and judge for yourself if your voice sounds freer and more energised.

Move the furniture out of the way and create enough space to be able to walk around and swing your arms safely.

Exercises for releasing Sound

QR Exercise 1

Stand upright with your feet a little apart, put your arms out to one side, stretch them up, then let them swing right down to the floor, bending your trunk down with them, then swing them up again to the other side. The really important thing to remember is that when you swing over forwards you must let your head and shoulders go completely – feel as much weight as possible when you swing down, so that the downswing impels the movement up to the other side. Do this once to get the idea of the movement. Think of a puppet with broken strings.

Now, as you take your hands up to one side, draw breath in; as you swing down, let the breath out making the sound 'AAAY', speaking it quite loudly, then swing up to the other side and breathe in. Swing down again saying the vowel 'I', allowing the energy of the downswing to expel the vowels. Do this at an easy pace, several times.

Rest for a moment. Then do the same thing again but this time speaking a few lines of a nursery rhyme or some months of the year on each swing, really allowing the sound to come out and making sure the neck, head and shoulders fall forwards completely free. Try 4 or 5 swings, with text, in this manner.

Immediately you have done this, repeat the few lines of the nursery rhyme again without the swinging, just standing still. Do you hear a difference from your normal restricted and under-energised voice?

QR Exercise 2

March around the room rather in the manner of a child, lifting up your knees (if you are able) and swinging your arms loosely and energetically. Once you've got into a rhythm and have created some energy and purpose, start chanting a nursery rhyme.

Voice

> Jack and Jill went up a hill
> To fetch a pail of water.
> Jack fell down and broke his crown
> And Jill came tumbling after.

Repeat this a couple of times and then stand still and just recite the same nursery rhyme. Does your voice sound more free and alive?

Exercise 3
You can also try star jumps while reciting a nursery rhyme, really pushing your arms and legs out, and then again stand still and listen to how your voice sounds when you stand still.

Why does this work?
Focussing on your voice can sometimes create more tension, so distracting yourself through movement and chanting can allow your voice to respond naturally, producing a freer and more natural sound. You are also breathing more fully because of the physical exertion and that breath can be harnessed to power the voice when the physical activity stops.

The same freeing thing happens if you do star jumps while practising your summing up speech – leap, really pushing your arms up and out, and then speak standing still. In court you then recall the quality of your voice while rehearsing and allow the muscle memory to work. In fact, any movement while working on speech is useful – even walking around the room with purpose or jogging. In everyday life we very rarely speak without some movement. The very act of standing formally in court does seem to inhibit many voices but you have to work against the physical restrictions affecting the voice.

Obviously you may struggle to find a private space before appearing in court where you can warm up and increase your vocal energy. The trick is to think back to when you were doing these exercises and creating a richer, more energised voice and tell yourself to recreate that sound. On voice workshops I can often help people produce a stronger voice by simply asking for 'more'. Everyone can always find more!

Energy in words

If you feel you need a more dynamic delivery it is also worth thinking about the energy in individual words. Sometimes presentations can sound particularly boring because the speaker uses too much jargon or dry, technical language. Even highly experienced speakers or actors struggle to make dull language sound interesting. Try reading out loud some of the following words. Put an action to the words to release the energy that matches them.

> Bounce bash crash explode gesture hit jog jump kill kick
> lob pull push press punch rush rage ram slice twist throw

How to speak at the right pace

Pacing is how fast or how slow you are speaking at any given moment. Too slow can be boring, but there are some exceptions where a slow delivery is vital. One of those is in court because of the necessity of effective delivery of important information and where the judge or shorthand writer needs to take notes. If you speak too quickly in court, you are liable to be told to slow down to accommodate a shorthand writer, or to enable the sheriff to take notes.

Most people speak too quickly and get away with it in general conversation, but in more formal situations, such as in court, the need to speak more slowly and deliberately is paramount. In fact a court in the USA did some research on this by talking to court reporters and the answer was this: "Most attorneys need to learn to speak more slowly and distinctly, especially with the new 'real time' transcripts. There's only one chance to get it right. This is a real basic skill that is often overlooked."

There are many reasons why speaking at a pace which is easy to follow is important:
> Fast talkers give the jury no time to think and to process vital information.
> Fast talkers make it impossible for the judge to make notes.
> Fast talkers can appear more insincere or nervous.
> Not everybody thinks as quickly as you do.

Before you start trying out exercises there are a few things which might help you.

Start listening to talk shows on the radio. Note the differences in pace used by the contributors and see how the different styles affect you. How easy is it to follow the arguments? What opinion of the speakers do you reach, based on their pace?

Then ask someone to tell you a story. As they tell you their story, take detailed notes as if you were a judge. It won't be long before you realise how difficult it is to keep up with someone speaking naturally.

That word 'naturally' is the key here. It's not natural to stand up and speak in court. It requires a different set of skills from ordinary day-to-day conversation, one of which is to be aware of how many people have to follow what you are saying. So, armed with your knowledge of how difficult it is to make detailed notes when the speaker isn't taking that into consideration and your new awareness of the power of a deliberate style of delivery, you now might want to set about creating a new professional voice.

So how do you change your habitual speed?

Breathing
Take the time to take a full breath before you even speak. Take a full breath between phrases and sentences. This will stop the sense of everything feeling rushed. The added bonus of taking a full breath is that this full breath may stop you inserting 'ums' and other fillers if you just allow yourself to take the time to take this breath instead of making a random noise. This full breath gives you thinking time as well. As you can see there are many good reasons to consider breathing fully, as well as it helping those of you who speak too quickly.

Shaping the words fully
If you have tried out the voice warm-up exercises you will have discovered that you need to take more time if you want to have clearer speech.

Posture
You may be helped by checking out your posture as detailed in an earlier exercise. There's no doubt that standing in a balanced, anchored position seems to send a message to the brain that you are more in control and this may stop you feeling over-anxious which your speech delivery may mirror. Certainly, leaning forward tends to make delivery faster.

Voice

Attitude

Some people speak rapidly because they feel they are not worth listening to, so they rush in order not to take up time. You need to feel you have something worth saying in order to fully commit to what you are saying and to take the time to do so. Remember that you are representing your client. You are his or her voice and you need to be listened to.

Facts and figures

Much of court work is in the detail. Facts are important: dates, location, time, numbers and key persons. Get used to putting in a brief pause before a fact.

Count your words per minute

Normal speech is around 170-180 words a minute. Check out your rate of speech and then try to bring the count down to 120-130 words a minute. This is the speed suggested for public speaking.

Flowing exercise QR

Use your arm to conduct yourself in a different rhythm: slowly, gently and smoothly use your hand as a baton to establish a side-to-side movement. Keep your arm and hand fairly relaxed and fairly near your body. Start talking, and you will find it almost impossible to speak rapidly while your arm is conducting in a leisurely manner.

One word at a time exercise

This is a useful exercise if you run all your words together.

Choose a short piece of text with which you are familiar or use the above sentence to start yourself off. Say out loud the first word. Really commit to it. Say it as clearly and confidently as you can. Only move on to the second word if you are satisfied with your delivery of the first word. Don't stint on the shorter words either: 'a', 'or ', 'at', 'if' and so on give great sense to any argument. When you have tried out 3 or 4 words individually then attempt to say them as a phrase, but still giving them full value and importance.

Voice

Marking Up Exercise QR

This is a useful exercise if you have to read out loud. But it can also be used as an exercise to help you control your rate of delivery and mark what is important, something you may not have been doing if you speak at a constant and fast rate.

Neither Ronnie nor I would advocate reading out prepared speeches so use this more as an exercise to train your brain in how to use the pause, with the hope that when delivering a speech without notes you will still retain some control over delivery.

Read a passage out loud a couple of times until you are familiar with it. Then mark in pauses where you feel they would help the sense of the passage. Remember, your listeners have not heard this before and they need guidance. Place a slash (/) where you want a brief pause. If you feel you need a slightly longer pause then mark the place with //. Similarly if you really want a dramatic pause mark the page with ///. Practise reading out loud following these marks. This should help you slow your delivery rate and consider the audience.

If you start trying out some of the above exercises you will notice a change in your speech. It may feel unnatural and too slow. However, reassure yourself that you are now speaking at the right pace for court work. If it doesn't feel unnatural, then you have probably reverted back to your original fast speed! Speaking more slowly will help your listeners and will also help your image, as you will sound more authoritative.

Using the pause shows that you are at ease with yourself. It also stops you sounding impulsive and will add more weight to your speech. Pausing at the end of a key point helps the listener to know where one thought ends and another begins. Pausing also allows listeners to reflect on what you are saying. They are staying connected to you rather than being left behind. If you dash on to a new point while they are still considering the previous one you will be out of synch.

Use variety of pace in your speech. Some points need a measured, deliberate delivery, almost emphasising word by word. Other pieces of information lend themselves to a more enthusiastic and lively delivery. It is variety which keeps your listeners engaged and it is variety which serves to emphasise something vital in your speech.

You could refer back to the 2 courtroom speeches in this chapter and use the marking up exercise to see how that affects your delivery. By now you should be working towards shaping all the sounds in speech and using an appropriate pace.

How to add variety to your delivery

Lord Chief Justice, Lord Judge of Draycote[55], has been reported as saying that young people make bad jurors because they find it hard to concentrate for long periods. He went on to say that they are unable to listen to complex arguments in a courtroom. I think it's fair to say that most people these days are not used to listening for long periods of time without entertainment or commercial breaks. Even commercials are shorter, based on new attention span research which shows that the average commercial has gone from 60 seconds in the 1950s to 15 seconds today. Writers of soap operas know this and write with that in mind. With this knowledge, court practitioners really need to be aware of using their voice to help to keep the interest of their listeners.

Vocal variety increases arousal and attention

This means having a voice not just with the attributes mentioned previously (clarity, energy and pace,) but also using the skills of actors and great orators. Let's have a look at some of them.

Pitch
The easiest skill to add to basic communication is the use of variety of pitch.

Put simply, pitch is the highness or lowness of the speaking voice. Pitch movement within a word is known as inflection, while pitch movement over phrases is intonation.

---

[55] Voir Dire Interview. The view from the other side. Litigation section of the Utah State Bar. Voir Dire volume 2, number 2 1997
Lord Chief Justice of Draycote. *The Telegraph* 06 November 2008. By Christopher Hope, Home Affairs Editor.

Pitch is also the musicality of the voice: how much the voice reflects the emotion of what is being said. Having a broader range allows more subtleties of thought and emotion to be expressed. It's also useful in marking changes in thought or facts. You move, as it were, from one paragraph to another. By changing pitch from higher to lower or vice versa, you are signalling to the listener that some change has occurred and you are drawing their attention to an episode or fact which demands their attention. All listeners drift off but they can be returned to the talk by using the simple trick of changing pitch.

Research has shown that top of the list of irritating vocal qualities is a monotonous tone. These are speakers who drone on with no variety in their voice. This is a perfect style to help babies fall asleep but does a lawyer no favours. Even the most dramatic prose will fail to make its mark if delivered in a flat voice. Be considerate of those who have to listen to you by making your voice more interesting.

An exercise to open up variety of pitch

A very basic vocal exercise to open up a wider variety of pitch in your voice is this one called The Siren. While saying 'Whoo', glide a siren sound from your lowest sound to your highest and then reverse the siren. Don't strain. I think it's also helpful to accompany the sound with the physical action of raising your arm while the siren moves up and lowering your arm while the siren descends.

You will also become more aware of your voice by reading children's stories out loud. By slightly exaggerating the extremes of pitch you will be accessing areas of your voice that you may not necessarily have used for a while. Feel free to add large gestures too as this will free your voice and make it more expressive.

Another exercise is to pick up the newspaper and mark any article with a pencil where you feel you might want to change pitch, either due to certain facts or a change of emotion or because you have a shift of mood or subject. You can devise your own system to cover pitch going up or down.

You can also go back to the 'marking up' exercise mentioned under the section on pace and add some further marks of your own devising to represent a change of pitch.

Another aspect of pitch which must be mentioned as it is a modern phenomenon is the younger lawyers' habit of adding an upward inflection at the end of sentences. It sounds irritating and questioning at inappropriate points and can make the speaker sound unsure. A court lawyer should always know when he or she wants to make an inquiry and at that point the voice should have an upward inflection. Otherwise it must be eliminated.

Male and female voices – differences in pitch

Due to the physical structure of the vocal chords, men and women have voices with distinctively different pitch. We expect women to have generally lighter, higher voices than men. However, a note of caution: some young female lawyers still seem to hold on to the breathy, girly, high-pitched voices which served them well as teenagers, along with girly body language, but when in court they lack gravitas. (Naturally high voices will also become higher if the speaker is more anxious than usual.)

There are exercises which can help to lower your voice but there is no such thing as a quick fix. There are physical and psychological reasons why we have the voices we have and these can be related to attitudes of parents and peers and events in our past. A serious decision to repeatedly and regularly work on a voice is the only way to effect any noticeable change.

Tone of voice

Tone is an emotion registered in your voice such as warmth and friendliness or detachment and efficiency.

As with everything else to do with the voice, the whole body is involved. Most people think that communication is centred around the mouth and throat, but think back to when you've seen someone extremely angry or upset and recall their posture, body language and energy.

The tone you use has to match the message and mood of the words. Inserting changes of tone just for variety's sake would not sound sincere. Ask yourself what you want your listeners to 'feel' as a result of what you are saying. You should then find that your vocal expression will be driven by your connection to what you are saying.

Voice

Exercise to work on changing the tone of your voice QR

This exercise will help you change your tone of voice at will. Practise this at home as it requires you to engage physically and mentally for the voice to change.

You may want to sound more authoritative. Think of a mental image to reflect this word. You may imagine an army officer or a sports coach or your boss. Now think of the body language of this persona. If I were to choose to be a sports coach I would sit with a relaxed but energised bearing and a strong gaze. Now I choose a word to mirror this image – power or respect. With the mental image and posture in place, say the word 3 times with 100% commitment. Then with that new tone of voice speak a line of your closing argument and listen to the difference. In the future just picture your mental image and the voice should be in place when you next need to sound more authoritative.

Let's look at sounding more warm. Again think of a mental image. It could be of a mother and child or a close friend. Your body language should be relaxed, and it helps to smile. The word to match to this scenario would be tender. Say the word 3 times then segue into a piece of your own speech which requires a softer touch.

Volume

It goes without saying that you need to be heard in court. Bear in mind that your audience may be looking down while making notes, may be listening unwillingly or may be finding the proceedings hard to follow and you can see that at the very least they shouldn't have to strain to hear what you are saying.

There are a few reasons why speakers may speak too quietly: cultural, social, familial and habitual factors may be at work. It is often because the speaker hesitates to make definite statements and holds back from commitment. Sometimes the speaker is just tired.

The voice is powered by the breath. Go back to the chapters on posture, relaxation and breathing as most problems with volume can be attributed in some part to these areas.

Voice

However the following skills can help a voice to sound bigger:

- Speaking at the right pace.
- Fully shaping vowels and consonants.
- Using a greater range of pitch.
- Using range and clarity for emphasis rather than volume.
- Using pauses effectively.

An exercise to help with awareness of the necessity of volume
For this exercise you need a partner and to be able to work in a large room.

> Stand back to back in the middle of the room and decide who is A and who is B.
> A starts the exercise by speaking a sentence. B replies.
> Then take a step away from each other, stand still and repeat the same sentences. Keep going until both participants are really quite a distance away from each other and still speaking the same sentence while facing in the opposite direction. It will become apparent that subtle changes of delivery are required if the other person is to receive the message easily. If you look at the list above, most or all of the suggestions would be required for clarity; that, and a further injection of energy.

Apart from having to be heard in court, experienced speakers use varying levels of volume to keep the interest of the listener. If the audience is drifting off, their attention may be brought back to the speaker if there is a change of volume. The listener will be aware that something different is happening if the speaker's voice goes from very soft to considerably louder.

Obviously you can also use volume to affect the mood of what you are saying. A quieter delivery might be more suitable when describing something horrific or moving. With reference to the speeches earlier in this chapter, I would instinctively quieten my voice to deliver the final sentence in *Adam's Rib* whereas I'd be more inclined to raise the volume to deliver the final sentence in the second piece, *An Ideal Husband*.

Again this is something you might want to set down in the Marking Up Exercise while you are in the process of learning all the vocal skills.

Accent

Just a few words about accent. Many lawyers approach me with concerns about their accents. In this day and age it is not necessary to speak only the Queen's English or Received Pronunciation. However, my only note re regional accents is to check for clarity and make sure that local expressions or dialect don't creep in.

If you do choose to change or modify your accent it will take a lot of time and motivation as your mouth and speech organs have been used to being placed in specific positions reinforced by a solid muscle memory which will be hard to change and may in fact distract you. Under stress the original accent may appear. By all means tidy up a few impenetrable sounds but I wouldn't advise a wholesale vocal make-over.

I think it would be fair to say that you might not be taken seriously if your grammar is poor. This is noticeable for example in the Central Belt of Scotland where I have heard in court "I done that", "Youz will appreciate" and "I have went". Use of these expressions will strike a discordant and distracting note, and will announce to the court that you are a sloppy and ungrammatical thinker, thereby undermining trust in the argument you are presenting.

Last words on The Voice

Every one of you can have a professional voice. I've seen so many people on my courses who tell me that they don't like their voices, or that they can't be heard and so on, but who, with some effort and understanding of what makes a voice easy to listen to, produce a lively free sound. However it's one thing to 'find' a voice when working with me and quite another to keep this new energised lively voice. The only way is practise practise practise. Try and approach this practice with a lightness of touch. Find the fun in the exercises and enjoy the sounds that you discover.

Suggested reading

Any of these books opened at random will offer you quality. Read anything out loud and get used to hearing and enjoying your voice.

>The New Oxford Book of English Verse
>The Penguin Book of Twentieth-Century Speeches
>Thinker, Failure, Soldier, Jailer – an anthology of great Lives in 365 days
>The Collected works of William Shakespeare
>Any of the novels of Charles Dickens.

19 BODY LANGUAGE

"I often feel that people don't take me seriously."

Body language affects how people see you and it also affects how you feel about yourself.

In this chapter I'll be looking at:

- What your body language says about and to you
- How to find a position of neutrality
- What negative body 'tics' you may have
- What to do with your hands

What your body language says about and to you

Not only are you making an impression on your audience by the way that you sit or stand, but you are affecting how you feel about yourself. Some interesting research has proven that adopting a 'power stance' can raise your testosterone and lower your cortisol levels. You are literally chemically changed. The rise in testosterone is linked to adaptive responses to challenges, useful when thinking on one's feet in court, while the lowering of the stress hormone cortisol helps to rein in the Fight or Flight response. Harvard Business School's Amy Cuddy and Columbia's Dana Carney have published research which shows that holding a 'power stance' for only 1 minute can effect these changes.[56]

---

[56] Amy J.C. Cuddy. Associate Professor of Business Administration, Hellman Faculty Fellow Harvard.
Dana R Carney. Assistant Professor University of California, Berkley CA TED talks. Global 2012 www.ted.com/talks/amy_cuddy_your_body_language_shapes_who_you_are.html

Body Language

What is a power stance? QR

A typical power stance is the alpha male position, with legs akimbo, pelvis jutting out and hands on hips. (This is not the position for court work – use only as an exercise). The key factor here is about occupying space, either sitting down or standing up.

For those of you starting out and feeling unconfident, this might be worth working on. In any difficult situation, for example the first time in court or going for an interview, it is possible to change a stressful situation to one in which you feel mentally and physically prepared simply by changing your stance. You will increase confidence and feel more powerful. Try and keep a generous imaginary amount of space around you.

Conversely, adopting a low status and closed position lowers testosterone and raises cortisol. In the short term you are presenting a weak image but the long-term damage is considerable with chronic negative health outcomes.

Women in particular adopt the **low-power stance**. It's not uncommon to see young female lawyers closing down their bodies to take up the smallest amount of space, with feet entwined and arms and hands clasped demurely in front of them. **QR**

Humans and other animals express power through open, expansive postures, and they express powerlessness through closed ones.

The less space you occupy the more you are indicating that you are insignificant. In court you want to be able to reassure those around you that you are up to the job. Don't let negative body language sell you short.

How to find a position of neutrality

I would advocate learning to find a neutral stance. Look at the chapter on posture. Get used to standing up and checking what your body is doing. Don't feel rushed into leaping to your feet and plunging into the business of the day. Take that moment to get comfortable and to eliminate those tell-tale signs of anxiety or low status. Are your feet shoulder-width apart? Are your shoulders relaxed? Are your knees soft? Are you taking up the right amount of room? Do you feel balanced and comfortable?

Check also that you are not placing your body slightly sideways. This could be read as an inability to face the world and could look defensive or timid. Face the jury or witness straight on.

If you have to walk to a podium, don't betray your lack of confidence by shuffling or looking down. If you have managed to achieve good posture when standing, keep that feeling of length in the spine while walking. Look to where you are heading and walk with purpose. A lawyer in court has to 'own' the space, rather as an actor does on stage. Your 'performance' starts before you open your mouth. Actually your performance starts before you enter the court and doesn't finish until you leave the building.

> **A useful tip to 'owning' the courtroom is to go to the room beforehand and make yourself comfortable with it. Walk around it, saying to yourself 'This is my space'. 'I have earned the right to be here.'**

If you can at least adopt this neutral stance, you will not be judged negatively. You can then, if you feel like it, adopt a slightly more confident position. The trick to that is to take up slightly more room, either when sitting or standing. Just open up the stance and feel more expansive.

> **A good exercise to try out at home is to walk around the largest room you have, with your arms outstretched, really owning the space. Walk with energy. Imagine that you are larger than you are. Imagine you are someone of authority. Then drop the arms and hold on to the feeling that you had when your arms were extended. You should feel 'larger'.**

Your body language needs to send a subliminal message. What image do you want to project? Most lawyers reply to that by suggesting, *looking confident, professional, prepared* and *exuding the expectation of winning their case*. These words make sense and indeed '*exuding the expectation of winning*' can be hugely helped by good posture as research has shown that 92 per cent of people found it easier to feel more positive while sitting or standing upright. Be aware as the day goes on and the courtroom warms up that you could well end up in a slumped position, projecting the wrong message, either that of defeat or exhaustion or boredom or indeed of arrogance. There is no doubt that the words chosen above require an on-going awareness of energy.

I'm sure most of you would agree that a neutral position is the correct one to take in your professional capacity. However, no matter how hard we work to assume that image we often betray our deeper anxieties through negative body language. Check the following list to see if any of them are familiar. If you do recognise that you slip up in more than one of these areas, don't try to eliminate them all at once. Just focus on the worst offender and start with that.

Take comfort in knowing that if you feel motivated to do so you *can* change negative body language.

What negative body 'tics' you may have

Head nodding. You may want to encourage a witness to tell their story and a natural way of doing this is to nod at the beginning of an examination-in-chief. But be careful not to repeat this throughout the examination. You might well be accused of leading the witness. In any event repeated head nodding can make you look submissive and less authoritative.

Girlie behaviour. If it's been pointed out to you that you fiddle with your hair, smile too much or stand in a cute manner with one of your feet turned in, then stand in front of a mirror and practice standing still and centred and then compare that to the 'girlie' stance. The latter stance is not exuding gravitas. Learn to be still.

Laddish behaviour. You may be overcompensating physically by widening your stance, and sticking your chest out. This may make you feel more confident but could make you look arrogant and intimidating. Watch this physical arrogance when walking as well. It won't do you any favours to be seen to be strutting into the court. Watch what message you are sending out too if you choose to sit, legs spread wide, hands folded behind your head, surveying the world as if you feel superior to those around you.

Pen fiddling. You may like holding a pen if you worry about what to do with your hands but the pen may become distracting. Jurors have been known to become fascinated by what an advocate does with their props and indeed set bets with each other as to how often the pen is tapped or twirled. Practice talking at home while sitting on your hands. You may find that your focus improves and that you speak more fluently.

Head tilts. Tilting your head to one side can make you look sympathetic and that has its use in the courtroom. Too much head tilting can look weak, as it is associated with low credibility because you may look confused. Try keeping the head in a neutral position. This is a trait more often seen in women.

Too much movement. Try to look calm and contained. Avoid shuffling around or fussing with your papers and gown.

Throat clearing. Anxiety can dry up saliva production and the throat will feel scratchy, resulting in irritating repeated throat-clearing. Take regular sips of water.

Lectern hugging. The lectern is there to hold your papers. It's not there for you to hide behind. Beware that you don't become 'smaller' if you do choose to stand behind it. Try standing to the side of it and use the space around it. Look at ease in this available space. If you do choose to use the lectern for security, check from time to time that you're not gripping tightly. This will make your shoulders hunch up and tighten your vocal chords, making you sound tense.

Lip biting. You are probably not aware that you are doing this. It's often a nervous tic from childhood. It's mannerisms like this that require a good friend to watch you in court and report back. Practise talking at home in front of a mirror, keeping an eye on your face, repeating to yourself when you pause, to *relax* and stay *calm*.

Nervous hands. Running your hands through your hair, or adjusting papers because your hands need to be doing something betray anxiety. If you are aware of this happening, put your 'busy' hand in your pocket to try and break the habit.

Frowning. Some people frown when they are concentrating. This could be read negatively as uncertainty or anger. Your voice will also be affected by the tension in your forehead, sharpening the tone of your voice.

Mouth tightening. This is a very common betrayal of tension. Consciously relax your face before making any presentation so that you can look at ease. Try keeping your lips slightly apart to prevent your mouth tightening.

Feet tapping. Nothing betrays our anxiety more than our feet. Do you have one foot poised up in the air as if wanting to leave the court? Do you shift from foot to

Body Language

foot which makes *you* look shifty? When you feel you are on shaky ground intellectually your body will probably betray that by excessive foot shuffling. Anchor those feet and feel secure. Be aware also that when sitting those feet can still keep moving. You may tap your feet or your legs may swing, sending out the wrong message as well as being distracting to others.

Eyes down. There is a certain amount of comfort in checking your notes. However they can also be a security blanket and take away from real contact with the witness. When you look down you lose control and status so keep these 'breaks' as short as possible. Your voice will also struggle to have any power if your eyes are directed downwards as well and you will narrow your world down to your papers. Overall you will not look prepared. Avoiding eye contact may also suggest that you can't cope with confronting a witness and you will lose credibility.

Listening exercise. One of the reasons that people look down is because they are looking at their next question. Ronnie has already given reasons why this is not a good idea in his chapter on cross-examination. Prepared questions are a security blanket but the problem is that you have no idea what the witness is going to say next so you cannot rely on *your* next question being relevant.

The key thing here is to learn how to listen.

I think it's fair to say that most of us don't listen fully. We anticipate what the other person is going to say and start to shape our own response. The following exercise will help you listen right to the *end* of what the speaker is saying. Try this out with a partner.

One of you is A and the other is B. A starts any general conversation. Choose a general topic like a recent holiday, travel or moving house. B listens intently and must not interrupt. When A has finished what they want to say, B then uses the last few words of A's final sentence to start their reply. A then listens and has to use the final 3 or 4 words of B's part of the conversation.
It will look like this....

Body Language

A   It was a great summer so I took the family *to the beach*.

B   *To the beach.* Wish I could have done the same but I was *stuck at work*.

A   *Stuck at work*? That's a shame. Were you not *due a holiday*?

B   *Due a holiday?* I certainly was but we're *really short staffed*.

A   *Really short staffed* seems a bit unfair on you when you are carrying such a workload. If you do get away you must try and get *up to Balmedie*.

B   *Up to Balmedie.* What's so special about *Balmedie?*

A   *Balmedie* has the most wonderful sand dunes and the kids loved playing on them.

This is obviously not natural speech but it will draw your attention to whether you are fully listening or not. You can progress from general conversation to practising questioning a witness. Use the same technique. Do not allow yourself to reply until you have heard and used the last few words of the other person. When you think you are beginning to listen more fully, then you can stop being as precise in the use of the other person's exact words.

Not only is this useful in court, but if you are meeting a client your listening skills will be improved and your client will be grateful for being listened to thoroughly.

What to do with your hands

As I've been saying in previous chapters, the body and voice are connected. It's not natural to stand stiffly without any movement in your arms and hands. It's very hard to add life and vigour to a voice if the body is constrained. However, it's about getting the balance while working in court. Keep your arms by your side and only consider using them when the impulse to move them matches what you are saying. Use them to add punch to a powerful word or statement for example. Use them to add emphasis. What I'm suggesting is that you use them when it feels natural to do so but to watch out that you're not waving your arms around in a generalised manner.

Body Language

Another point regarding hands is that you should try to keep them visible as much as possible. Psychologically you will be showing that you are honest and open especially if you show an open palm.

An exercise to show how movement affects your voice

Read the following paragraph a couple of times to yourself so that you understand the content.

Firstly read it out loud while standing as stiffly as you can, staring straight ahead and with an expressionless face. Listen to what you sound like.

> "I take the war list and I run down it, name after name, which I cannot read, and which we who are older than you cannot hear without emotion; names which will be only names to you, the new College, but which to us summon up face after face, full of honesty and goodness, zeal and vigour, and intellectual promise; the flower of a generation, the glory of England; and they died for England and all that England stands for."
>
> (Master of Caius: *Exhortation to the 1919 Cambridge University Freshman Class. Chariots of Fire* 1981)

Now relax your body, stand with feet shoulder-width apart, put some energy and expression on to your face and read it out loud, using as many gestures as you feel like including. Keep trying this out, using different movements and facial expressions and you should discover a broader range to your voice. What happens to your voice if you raise your eyebrows? What happens if you have a broad smile on your face? What happens when you frown and lean forward? What happens when you sweep your arm around as if gesturing to the whole court? What adds brightness to the tone? What gives your voice a more serious tone?

The other thing to notice is what happens to the speed of your delivery if you speed up the action of your arms. If you are someone who has too rapid a rate of speech, practice moving your hands and arms very slowly. It's almost impossible to speak quickly if you are gesturing slowly.

Gestures

Generally you will look more confident if your gestures are smooth and controlled. It's worth considering this particularly at the start of your presentation, as it will set the tone and style for what is to follow. It will also allow your listeners to get used to your style and to your voice and to tune in, as it were.

The other thing to bear in mind is that gestures which might seem expansive enough out of the court may not register in the court itself. This takes us back to the point at the beginning of this chapter – take up more room than may feel natural. Use the whole arm if you want to make a gesture, not just the hand and wrist. You are more likely to be mean with your movement if you are inhibiting your arms. Short jerking actions will make you look nervous, and again the physical action may affect the voice. It's not unreasonable to see that jerky movements could make the voice sound tight and brittle whereas a fully executed gesture will underpin what the message is, especially if it is a vehement point.

When not speaking you might find it useful to keep your arms loosely by your side or, arms bent, your hands lightly touching at waist height. Try and avoid hands clasped any lower, or hands clasped behind the back. If you place your hands in too low a position you will be lowering your status as it is a submissive position. It also means that when you feel you want to make a gesture your arms and hands have further to travel, whereas if you have your hands clasped loosely and across your abdomen, it's a smoother movement and you are in a position of readiness.

People-watching is a useful exercise. You will see how much movement we all make when relaxed and committed to what we are saying. You will see how much authority someone has by the way they stand and walk and so on. Watch people whom you admire in court and pick the best bits of their style and use them! And practise, practise, practise.

20 PREPARATION

"It's not great at the start but then after a moment I settle down."

Preparation is a somewhat general term. Ronnie has covered what he would expect the preparation to be in terms of briefs etc., but I would like to look at what you can do to prepare your body and your mind. The chapter on Voice will suggest ways of preparing your voice.

In this chapter I'll be looking at:

- The importance of warming up
- Suggested exercises prior to court

In addition, I have put together two warm-up routines. The first one is the **Advocacy Quickstart Routine**. This should be used before *every* public presentation or court appearance. It will wake you up, mentally, physically and vocally.

The second set of exercises is the **Advocacy Core Practice Routine**. I would suggest that if you find time to carry this out once a week, you will be reinforcing fundamental performance skills.

The importance of warming up

In my experience, most people prepare their material but they leave the rest of their performance to chance. However, most of us know that we are judged by more than what we say so it's as well to make sure that we are giving ourselves our best chance from the outset.

Preparation

If you have ever played sport you will understand that warming up prepares you physically and mentally for the game or match which is to follow. If you are anxious before a game, warming up will help to put nerves in their place. If you feel under-energised, a warm up will help you move up a gear and actually create energy. If you feel unfocussed or distracted the warm up will correct that. So you might find it helpful to think of the courtroom as a tennis court or a stage, both of which require that you be as prepared as fully as you can be to give yourself the best chance.

Actors playing leading roles in Shakespearean plays need to be fit. These are demanding parts, asking of these actors, energy, physical fitness and great breath control to allow the language to flow easily from their mouths and reach the audience in the Upper Circle.

Every lawyer I have ever trained benefits from any workout I have in my courses. Most people are nervous at the start of the session, which often mirrors how they feel in court. Most people have under-energised bodies and voices. Most people need to check where they are holding tension and pay attention to their posture. A warm up will address these issues.

Suggested exercises prior to court

Below, you will find two warm up routines. I recognise that most people don't have the time to do a thorough warm up, so exercise 1 (**Advocacy Quickstart Routine**) offers the minimum which might help prior to appearing in court or making a presentation.

The second set of exercises (**Advocacy Core Practice Routine**) offer a slightly fuller workout with the hope that the brain will recognise how different the body can feel with full preparation, and hold on to the memory of that relaxed and prepared state. You may also, by the time you have finished this book, have found other exercises which you feel are of more help to you. Substitute any of those until you have created your own tailor-made warm up. Some of the components may require that you pay more attention to them and others you may feel are less useful. For example if you know where you hold tension, then that would be an area that you should spend more time on. The full warm up should include a balance of physical, vocal and mental exercises.

Preparation

1. Pre-court Advocacy Quickstart Routine QR

(This will help to wake you up, physically, vocally and mentally as well as removing excess nerves.)

Walk briskly up and down the corridor or find the emergency stairs for some privacy. Walk with purpose. Psych yourself up with an internal running commentary. "This is going to go well", "I am creating energy", "I am preparing myself."

Or slap yourself gently all over – when you feel a tingle you can stop.

Shake out tension in your arms and legs. Stretch your face, and then squash it up. Blow out your lips like a horse. Hum a few bars of a well-known song.

Stretching Exercise

Stand with your feet shoulder-width apart. Stretch your arms out to the side, imagining that energy is flowing to your fingertips. Then stretch the arms upwards, stand on tiptoes and try to reach as high as you can. Then think of yourself as a puppet and imagine that someone has cut your strings which will allow you to collapse, with your head falling forwards gently, bringing your arms and spine with it until you are collapsed, like a rag doll, from the waist.

From this position, you will unfold yourself and come up slowly through the spine, vertebra by vertebra, until the shoulders fall into place naturally and finally the head will rise and be balanced at the top of the spine.

Recite slowly the following tongue twister to warm up the speech organs.

> My organs of articulation
> Were a definite vexation
> Till I said this silly rhyme
> Six times through.

2. The Advocacy Core Practice Routine QR

Shaking Exercise

Just loosely shake out the body, shoulders, hips, legs, feet, arms and hands. Imagine that you are shaking off all excess tension and flicking it or flinging it away.

Stretching Exercise

Stand with your feet shoulder-width apart. Stretch your arms out to the side, imagining that energy is flowing to your fingertips. Then stretch the arms upwards, stand on tiptoes and try to reach as high as you can. Then think of yourself as a puppet and imagine that someone has cut your strings which will allow you to collapse, with your head falling forwards gently, bringing your arms and spine with it until you are collapsed, like a rag doll, from the waist. Hang there gently for a beat or two enjoying the sensation of complete relaxation.

Next, hug yourself gently and breathe in deeply. You should feel the back opening. Take a few slow breaths. Then drop the arms so that they are hanging heavily, devoid of tension.

From this position, you will unfold yourself and come up slowly through the spine, vertebra by vertebra, until the shoulders fall into place naturally and finally the head will rise and be balanced at the top of the spine.

The above exercise is a favourite for all performers as it is calming.

By now you should be feeling both physically and mentally more relaxed. It may take some experience trying this out to really help you get to this state. In which case, repeat all of the above a couple more times until your body starts to feel the benefit.

Shoulders
Most of us carry much of our tension in our shoulders so you might find it helpful to work on the shoulders as well as doing the general stretching exercises.

Preparation

Stand with your feet shoulder-width apart, with soft knees. Shrug the shoulders up as closely to your ears as possible, while breathing in, then let the air out at the same time as dropping the shoulders. Repeat this a few times. Allow the shoulders to drop into position.

Again, standing with feet shoulder-width apart and with soft knees, take one arm and swing it in a wide circle. I find it helps to bounce the knees as well. Imagine that your joints are all made of honey so the movement of the shoulder is gentle and easy. Then repeat with the other arm.

The Face
Imagine that your face is made of putty. Make your hands into gentle fists, place them on your cheeks and draw them downwards, imagining that you are stretching the putty. This will have the effect of stretching the cheeks and pulling the jaw down. Repeat a few times until you feel that when your jaw springs back, it is not going back into such a tight position.

Pull your face in as if you wanted it to resemble a fist – scrunch it up and screw up your eyes. Then imagine that you are in a horror movie, making a silent scream – eyes wide and mouth open. Alternate between both extremes to waken up your whole face. You will feel more alert after that and if it's made you laugh, so much the better, as nothing relaxes one as much as laughing.

Imagine that you are a monkey and push your lips forward first, followed by the stretched grimace that monkeys make. Try this a few times, and then blow out your lips like a horse. Follow that with some air kisses as if you were at a first night party at the opera.

Voice warm up
Gently *hum* any song that comes easily to you. I use nursery rhymes but you can hum anything that you enjoy. Try a few different tunes so that there is a variety to the notes, which will help you use a good amount of your register.

Follow this by making the sound of a siren. You make the sound 'whoo' and glide from your lowest note to your highest note. Keep the sound nasal but don't force it.

Preparation

Speech warm up
The following sentences are to warm up your articulators so that you avoid mumbling. Both vowels and consonants are important if you want to have clear speech so work through the following, reading them out loud, slowly shaping all the sounds fully.

> A white witch watched a woebegone walrus winding white wool.

> Green tea ice cream is a treat to eat.

> Old folks row slowly.

> A big beetle bit a body in a big black bag.

> Many merry moments make Madge mischievous.

> A sick sparrow sang six sad spring songs sitting sheltering under a squat shrub.

> Three fluffy feathers fell from feeble Phoebe's fan.

> It's our duty to salute the new recruit.

> Todd placed the pot on the rock.

> A cup of creamy custard cook cooked for Cuthbert.

> A thin little boy picked six thick thistle sticks.

Mental preparation
Check that you are standing comfortably – feet shoulder-width apart, shoulders relaxed, eyes facing straight ahead, and finish this sequence by thinking of the right thought to take you into the courtroom. Find a sentence that works for you. Some suggestions – "I am fully prepared", "I am a professional and I can do this", "Now I'm ready."

Appendices - Exercises

EXERCISES

Once you have understood the exercises in context you will have identified the ones that will be most useful to you and can just go straight to them with your QR reader. All of the exercises available to watch are listed below.

Chapter 14 Anxiety

The Flower and the Candle breathing exercise QR

- Sit comfortably on an upright chair.
- Place your feet firmly on the ground.
- In your right hand you have your 'flower'.
- In your left hand you have your 'candle'.
- Bring the flower to below your *nose* and breathe in.
- Exhale steadily through the *mouth* towards the candle.
- Repeat a few times until you have a calm rhythm.
- Now place your hands loosely on your lap and repeat.

Chapter 15 Relaxation

Where do you hold tension? (You need a partner for this exercise) QR

- Write the parts of the body in a column down one side of a page.
- Find a comfortable seat and close your eyes.
- Put yourself back in time to when you were in a stressful situation.
- Your partner will now call out the parts of the body from the list.
- With each body part think back to how your body felt and describe that tension to your partner.

Exercises

- Your partner will make notes.
- Now repeat this exercise but this time thinking of a situation when you were very relaxed.
- Compare the descriptions of how your body felt when stressed versus relaxed.
- This will tell you where you hold the worst of your tension.

General relaxation exercise QR

- Stand with your feet shoulder-width apart.
- Your knees and thighs should be soft.
- Raise your arms above your head.
- Stretch towards the ceiling, without lifting your feet off the floor. Hold this for 20 – 30 seconds.
- Imagine that you are a puppet and someone is cutting the strings.
- First at the wrists so your hand flops over.
- Now at the shoulders so that your arms flop down by your side, feeling heavy.
- Now the string supporting your head is cut.
- Allow the weight of your head to make it flop over, falling forward and bringing the shoulders and back with it until you are bent over.
- Now bend your knees and just hang there with heavy head and arms.
- Hold this position for a short while. Come up if you feel dizzy.
- Remember to keep breathing.
- Then gently unfold, vertebra by vertebra from the base of the spine, until you are upright again.
- Allow the arms to hang free.
- Don't 'place' the shoulders. Allow them to settle on their own.
- Keep your eyeline ahead of you.
- The trick to this exercise is to take your time. If you unfold speedily you will feel no different at the end of this exercise.
- Try it out a few times until it feels leisurely and calming.

Exercises

Releasing tension in the face QR

- Scrunch up your face as if it were a fist, closed and tight.
- Then open the whole face by pretending that you are extremely surprised.
- Really open your eyes and mouth wider than normal.
- Now scrunch up the face again.
- Move from closed fist expression to surprised several times.

Chapter 16 Breathing

Exercise to check if the diaphragm is being engaged QR

- Lie on the floor with your head supported.
- Bend your knees.
- Place a heavy book on your midriff and breathe deeply.
- As you exhale suck your stomach in towards your spine.
- Try to empty your lungs of as much air as possible.
- You should see and feel the book rising and falling as you breathe in and out.

- If this isn't happening then in all probability you are breathing shallowly in the upper chest.
- It may take a while for the movement to shift from the upper chest to the belly area.

The Flower and the Candle exercise QR

- Sit comfortably on a simple chair, making sure your feet are planted firmly.
- Imagine that in one hand you are holding a flower with a wonderful rich scent.
- In the other hand you are holding a lit candle.
- Bring the hand with the flower up to just below your nose.

Exercises

- Breathe in the scent of your flower through your nose, imagining the scent going all the way down to your diaphragm.
- Then blow out calmly and steadily through your mouth towards your candle in the other hand.
- Keep this out-breath slow and steady.
- You want to picture making the flame flicker.
- It is this steady out-breath which will help you to feel calm.
- Once you feel you understand how this works you can replace your hands loosely on your lap.
- Now just imagine the flower and candle in front of you.

Moving from breathing into speaking exercise QR

- Breathe in through the nose and out through the mouth until a smooth and relaxed rhythm has settled.
- Then begin a mental count of inspiration and expiration. Count in for 3 and out for 3.
- Once you've got used to this, you can start to vary the count. Try aiming for a shorter count for the in-breath and a longer count for the out-breath. A count of 2 for inspiration and 4 for expiration is good to begin with.
- Check that the intercostal muscles are controlling the outgoing sigh, as this is the whole point of this exercise.
- Wait before you breathe in again so you can actually feel the impulse to take the next breath.
- As you start to become more comfortable with this exercise you could decrease the inspiration count and extend the expiration time. This now mirrors the pattern of breathing necessary for speech.
- Finally, repeat this exercise but vocalise the counting, starting at a low number and increasing to match your breath capacity.
- Finally, replace the external counting with some Nursery Rhymes so that you are relating connected speech to the outbreath.

Exercises

Chapter 17 Posture

Simple alignment exercise QR

- Stand with your feet shoulder-width apart.
- Shoulders should be dropped and relaxed.
- Your head should be balanced.
- Hug yourself with arms criss-crossed.
- Bend the knees gradually.
- Flop over from the waist.
- Breathe in deeply and feel your back open.
- Take in a few unhurried breaths.
- Drop the arms. You should look like a rag doll, heavy and limp.
- To work towards a standing position, straighten the knees.
- Come up slowly vertebra by vertebra from the base of the spine.
- Allow the shoulders to find their natural position.
- Imagine that your head is a balloon balancing lightly on your spinal column.
- From this upright position rise up on to the balls of your feet.
- Keep looking straight ahead.
- Now lower yourself down to balance equally on the whole foot.

Eyeline exercise QR

- Check your posture first.
- Place your eyes at a specific point at the other side of the room.
- Keep looking at that spot and walk with purpose towards it.
- Don't look away while walking.
- When you reach your destination - stop.
- Now let your eyes choose another spot elsewhere in the room.
- Turn the head in that direction.

Exercises

- Walk with purpose again to the new spot keeping your eyes fixed on where you want to be.
- Keep walking to new fixed points until it feels more natural to be looking ahead rather than at the floor.

How to walk correctly A QR

- Keep your back straight.
- Soften your knees and squeeze your buttocks.
- Imagine a string in the middle of the head pulling your head up. Then imagine someone pulling on the string.
- This impels you to start walking.

How to walk correctly B QR

- Lean against a wall.
- Put your feet shoulder width apart.
- Let the wall support you.
- Get balanced.
- Focus on your forehead.
- Now set off allowing the forehead to lead.

Chapter 18 Voice

Pre-vocal warm-up exercise QR

- Begin by screwing up your face as tight as you can. Hold for a few seconds and then let go. Repeat.
- Imagine you are holding something under your nose which has a revolting smell and wrinkle up your face in an exaggerated fashion, then let go.
- Now imagine that you are suddenly surprised – stretch open your mouth and eyes for a couple of seconds and then let go.

Exercises

- Imagine that your face is made of putty. Make gentle fists, place them against your cheeks and gently draw them down, imagining that you are stretching the jaw as the putty is pulled down. Repeat. You should feel that your jaw is less tight after this exercise.
- Imagine that you have a chocolate-covered toffee in your mouth. Chew it round and round in a relaxed but exaggerated manner. Then use your tongue to lick off the chocolate that has smeared onto your lips.
- Now imagine that you are a cat lapping up milk.
- Then blow your lips out as if you were a horse snorting. Repeat.
- Now make some energetic air kisses adding the accompanying sound 'Mwaah'.
- Finally, yawn while counting out 1, 2, 3. This should help to open up the throat.

The Cork Exercise – working towards clearer speech QR

"Consider this unfortunate woman's act as though you yourself had each committed it. Every living being is capable of attack, if sufficiently provoked. Assault lies dormant within us all. It requires only circumstances to set it in violent motion. I ask you for a verdict of not guilty. There was no murder attempt here, only a pathetic attempt to save a home."

Adam's Rib (1949 American film written by Ruth Gordon and Garson Kanin and directed by George Cukor.)

- Have an extract from a legal speech printed out in large font. *(see above)*
- Read it out loud.
- Now take a cork and place it horizontally between your teeth.
- Exert enough pressure to keep it in place at the front of the mouth.
- Read out loud again.
- Speak very slowly and shape every syllable in an exaggerated way.
- Now remove the cork and read the passage again.
- Feel and hear the difference.
- Repeat again if necessary.

Exercises

The Vowels exercise – working towards a more rounded sound QR

- Have an extract from a legal speech printed in large font.
- Read it out loud to familiarize yourself with the words.
- Put a mark above all the vowels in the words to guide you.
- Now read it out loud pronouncing only the *vowels*.
- Speak them the way they would sound.
- Take your time and exaggerate the vowels stretching them out.
- Make each vowel sound separate and distinct from its neighbour.
- You will sound strange but persevere.
- Finally, read the passage again re-instating the consonants.
- Can you hear that your speech is clearer?

Exercise for releasing sound 1 QR

- Stand upright with your feet hip-width apart.
- Stretch your arms up to one side.
- Then swing them right down to the floor, bending your trunk over with them and continue the swing up to the other side.
- Let your head and shoulders hang heavy while you do this.
- The downward action impels the movement up to the other side.
- Repeat a couple of times to get the feel of the momentum.
- Next, draw in a breath while you are stretched up.
- As you swing down and up, let the breath out making the sound 'AAAY', speaking with full energy.
- When you reach the other side repeat the action.
- Keep breathing at the top of the stretch and letting the sound out on the swing.
- You can vary the vowel sounds.
- Let the energy of the downswing expel the vowel sounds.

Exercises

- Rest for a moment.
- Then move from vowel sounds to speech, using a nursery rhyme or the months of the year.
- You will manage a few words per swing.
- Finally just stand still and speak the words of the nursery rhyme without the swinging of the torso and arms.
- Do you hear that your voice sounds more energised?

Exercise for releasing sound 2 QR

- March on the spot as if you were a child playing at soldiers.
- Lift up your knees and swing your arms loosely and energetically.
- Once you have created energy and purpose add speech.
- Start chanting a familiar nursery rhyme.
- Repeat this a couple of times keeping the energy up.
- Then stand still and immediately recite the poem again.
- Your voice should sound more free and alive.
- You could replace the rhyme with a legal speech.

Flowing exercise – to help control the pace of speech QR

- Stand with feet shoulder-width apart and with soft knees.
- Use your arm to conduct yourself in a different rhythm.
- Imagine it is a baton.
- Slowly and smoothly use your hand to establish a side-to-side movement.
- Keep your arm and hand fairly relaxed and close to your body.
- Start talking.
- You will find your speech should match the rhythm of the arm.

Exercises

Marking up Exercise – to help with use of the pause QR

- Read a passage out loud a couple of times.
- Now mark in pauses to help the listener follow the sense of it.
- Place a slash (/) where you want a brief pause.
- Place 2 slashes (//) if you feel you need a slightly longer pause.
- Place 3 slashes (///) if you want a dramatic pause mark.
- Now read the passage out loud again using these marks to guide you.
- Keep remembering that your audience has not heard this before.

Exercise to help to change the tone of your voice – to sound more authoritative QR

- Sit on a chair, well balanced with feet placed firmly on the floor.
- Think of a mental image to reflect the word *authoritative.*
- You may imagine an army officer or a sports coach.
- Now think of the body language of this persona.
- Try sitting with military bearing and strong unwavering gaze.
- Now choose a word to mirror this image – *power* or *respect.*
- Put the three together –posture, image and word.
- Say the word steadily three times with 100% commitment.
- Don't rush.
- Then say the word 3 times again but follow on with a line of your closing argument using the same *tone* of voice.
- In the future just picture your mental image and the voice should be in place when you next need to sound more authoritative.

Exercises

Chapter 19 Body Language

Power Stance QR

- Stand with feet wide apart.
- Raise your arms in the air or put your hands on your hips.
- Feel that you are powerful and taking up space.

Low status stance QR

(This is not something to work towards! Rather this is to identify if this feels habitual to you, so that you can rectify this.)

- Put your feet close together.
- Put your hands together in front of you.
- Your eyeline will be directed towards the floor.
- Tuck your shoulders in.
- Let your stomach feel slumped.

Chapter 20 Preparation

Pre-court Advocacy Quickstart Routine QR

(This will help to wake you up, physically, vocally and mentally as well as removing excess nerves)

- Walk briskly up and down the corridor or emergency stairs.
- Walk with purpose.
- Psych yourself up with an internal running commentary.
- Say to yourself "This is going to go well", "I am creating energy", "I am preparing myself."
- Slap yourself gently all over until you feel a tingling.
- Shake out tension in your arms and legs.
- Rotate your shoulders.

Exercises

- Stretch your face, and then squash it up.
- Blow out your lips like a horse.
- Stand with your feet shoulder-width apart.
- Stretch your arms out to the side.
- Imagine that energy is flowing to your fingertips.
- Then stretch the arms upwards.
- Stand on tiptoes and try to reach as high as you can.
- Think of yourself as a puppet and imagine that someone has cut your strings.
- You now collapse allowing your head to fall forwards gently.
- Let your arms and spine follow your head until you are collapsed.
- Hang loosely in this position bent over from the waist.
- Now unfold yourself and come up slowly through the spine, vertebra by vertebra.
- Let the shoulders fall into place naturally.
- Let the head balance at the top of the spine.
- Warm up your voice by humming a well-known tune.
- Recite the following tongue twister slowly and clearly.

>My organs of articulation
>
>Were a definite vexation
>
>Till I said this silly rhyme
>
>Six times through.

The Advocacy Core Practice Routine QR

- Just loosely shake out the body.
- Shake tension out of shoulders, hips, legs, feet, arms and hands. Imagine that you are flinging tension away.
- Stand with your feet shoulder-width apart.
- Stretch your arms out to the side.

Exercises

- Then stretch the arms upwards, stand on tiptoes and try to reach as high as you can.
- Then think of yourself as a puppet and imagine that someone has cut your strings which will allow you to collapse.
- Let your head fall forwards gently, bringing your arms and spine with it until you are collapsed, like a rag doll, from the waist.
- Hang there gently for a beat or two enjoying the sensation of complete relaxation.
- Don't forget to breathe through all this.
- Then drop the arms so that they are hanging heavily, devoid of tension.
- Now unfold yourself and come up slowly through the spine, vertebra by vertebra.
- Let the shoulders fall into place naturally.
- Finally the head will rise and be balanced at the top of the spine.
- In this relaxed neutral position move on to working on your shoulders.
- Stand with your feet shoulder-width apart, with soft knees.
- Shrug the shoulders up as closely to your ears as possible.
- Breathe in while you do so.
- Now breathe out and drop the shoulders at the same time.
- Repeat this a few times.
- Now take one arm and swing it in a wide circle.
- Bounce the knees gently at the same time.
- Imagine that your joints are all made of honey so the movement of the shoulder is gentle and easy.
- Then repeat with the other arm.
- Moving on to the face, imagine that it is made of putty.
- Make your hands into gentle fists.
- Place them on your cheeks and draw them downwards, imagining that you are stretching the putty.
- Repeat a few times until you feel that when your jaw springs back, it is not going back into such a tight position.

Exercises

- Pull your face in as if you wanted it to resemble a fist – scrunch it up and screw up your eyes.
- Then imagine that you are in a horror movie, making a silent scream with eyes wide and mouth open.
- Alternate between both extremes to waken up your whole face.
- Imagine that you are a monkey and push your lips forward first, followed by the stretched grimace that monkeys make.
- Try this a few times.
- Now blow out your lips like a horse.
- To warm up the voice, gently *hum* any song that comes easily to you. Then hum a different tune so that you are varying your vocal range.
- Follow this by making the sound of a siren.
- Make the sound 'whoo' and glide from your lowest note to your highest note.
- Keep the sound nasal but don't force it.
- To warm up the speech organs recite slowly and clearly the following tongue twisters:

   A white witch watched a woebegone walrus winding white wool.

   Green tea ice cream is a treat to eat.

   Old folks row slowly.

   A big beetle bit a body in a big black bag.

   A sick sparrow sang six sad spring songs sitting sheltering under a squat shrub.

   Three fluffy feathers fell from feeble Phoebe's fan.

   It's our duty to salute the new recruit.

   Todd placed the pot on the rock.

Exercises

> A cup of creamy custard cook cooked for Cuthbert.
>
> A thin little boy picked six thick thistle sticks.

Finally prepare yourself mentally

- Check that you are standing comfortably – feet shoulder-width apart, shoulders relaxed, eyes facing straight ahead.

- Finish this sequence by thinking of the right thought to take you into the courtroom.

- Find a sentence that works for you.

- Some suggestions:

    > "I am fully prepared",
    > "I am a professional and I can do this",
    > "Now I'm ready."

Exercises

Reading of Introduction of an Outline Submission by Dorothy Bain QC.

Voice extract only QR

I'm reading this speech considerably more slowly than it would be delivered in court. The reason for this is that if you are habitually a fast speaker you will help your brain by rehearsing this speech at my exaggerated slow tempo. Then when you next have to speak in court you may revert back to speaking closer to your normal rapid speed but hopefully with some control over the delivery.

OUTLINE SUBMISSIONS FOR THE PURSUERS

Catherine McGee & Ors –v- RJK Building Services Limited

Introduction

On 5th May 2008, the defenders erected bilateral internal bannisters (hereinafter handrail/s) over a staircase comprising 13 stairs within the property of the late Peter McGee and the first and second pursuer, Catherine McGee at 22 Mosesfield Street, Springburn, Glasgow (hereinafter "locus").

The manner in which the internal handrails were installed was negligent. This is accepted by the defenders. As a result of the defenders' negligence, it is alleged that on the morning of the 16th July 2009, the late Peter McGee fell down the stairs at the locus, sustaining severe injuries that resulted in his death two days later.

In this case the pursuers contend that at around 2.30 am on Friday 16th July 2009, the deceased got up out of bed and left the bedroom that he shared with his wife. Their bedroom was situated upstairs and he intended to go downstairs to the kitchen for a drink of water. He started to descend the stairs, holding onto the handrail with his left hand, when the handrail came away from the wall, causing the deceased to fall forwards down the staircase and eventually landing at the bottom of the stairs. The defenders plead that the accident occurred as a result of the deceased, perhaps being disorientated, losing his footing and then falling to the bottom of the stairs and in doing so, falling heavily against the bannister, injuring his chest and ribs. Further, the defenders also plead contributory negligence, averring on record that, the deceased failed to take care when he was descending the stairs.

Appendices - Shared Experience

(1) PERSONAL TIPS FROM PERFORMERS

    Harry Nicoll, Opera Singer
    Lucy Goldie, Actor
    Eliza Langland, Actor / Coach
    Jennifer Hainey, Actor
    Lyn Murray, Actor
    Sharon MacKenzie, Actor
    Thomas Walker, Opera Singer
    Greg Powrie, Actor
    Kirsty Wark, Journalist / Author
    John Jack, Actor / Coach

Actors and performers spend their whole working lives coping with performance anxiety. Indeed stage fright can often increase with experience. We all find ways to cope with this part of our job and you may be interested to read how other people who work in the public eye handle stress.

If nerves begin to take hold…..
BREATHE OUT.
Don't think about breathing IN but allow the breath to come up from the floor, through your hollow legs. This of course is not possible, but will help to stop you from breathing too high. Take your time. You are in control. Make sure your feet are firmly planted on the floor. Make sure that your knees and fingers/wrists are not locked and tense. If the fingers/wrists are locked, then the arms are locked, then the shoulders are locked and then you can't breathe freely. Wiggle your knees and fingers a bit to make sure that they are loose.

Harry Nicoll, Opera singer

Just before a performance I usually do some physical activity – to get out of my head if that makes sense. A kind of shake out to rid myself of nervous energy. And anything that reminds me of my physical strength too, like doing the plank or making bold solid movements through space. Knowing exactly what you are doing (what is coming step by step) is also helpful. I like to feel well rehearsed and ready for what lies ahead.

Lucy Goldie, Actor

'Softening the Gaze' helps me. This is the practice of using your peripheral vision when looking at an assembly of people. You can spook yourself simply by using a tight focus in your visual field but if you relax your visual field by allowing yourself to become aware of the walls, ceiling and floor around you it is physiologically impossible to be stressed. It's undetectable too. Nobody knows you're doing it. It engages the parasympathetic system. As does breathing of course.
www.wkeithward.com/articles/theeyeshaveit.pdf

Eliza Langland, Actor/Coach

Just breathe

Jennifer Hainey, Actor

Listen. Think. Respond

Freddy Robinson, Actor/Director

Trust yourself

Lyn Murray, Actor

To calm the flight or fight instinct, calm the triple warmer meridian which simply involves tracing the meridian backwards with your hand. Trace or stroke from the temple around your ear, down your neck, shoulder arm and off your ring finger. A shortcut and quick boost is to tuck your hair behind your ears – called a smoothie. You see people like Andy Murray do this action instinctively and there is no hair to tuck behind the ears! He is being instructed by his subconscious mind during interviews to keep calm.

Sharon MacKenzie, Actor

I remember having a chat with a famous opera singer who admitted to feeling nervous often. He said that what liberated him was "nerves are ego." He gave himself permission to not be perfect. To make a mistake in every performance but to do his best to do justice to the production/music/colleagues. Also if I feel distracted I focus on what is happening right now, not the tricky bit coming up, or the bit I screwed up a moment ago. To be totally in the moment takes away from the ego and these nerves.

Thomas Walker, Opera singer

Appendices - Shared Experience

Don't know if this is any use, but relaxation is key to any good performance/presentation I think. I have a mantra that I repeat to myself whenever nerves threaten and it is simply 'This is what I do.' Not rocket science but it serves to remind me that it is what I have trained to do, worked towards and this is my moment to relish every second.

Greg Powrie, Actor

In the run up to a major interview or discussion there are straightforward steps that I follow. Firstly, get the grooming out of the way. I cannot stress how important it is to feel comfortable and confident in your appearance. Nothing too tight, too fiddly, or too elaborate. Dress well and then forget it.
Ease yourself into your subject matter, reading, chatting and making notes and then settle down to proper homework - a mind map is often my starting point and then I straighten it all out - think about possible responses and traps. Finally you should have no more than an A4 of prompts, quotes, and questions. Then you should feel relaxed and on your game.

It is very important to give yourself time to absorb all this and then let it go. Take at least ten minutes before the interview - I do that in the makeup chair, or quietly in the studio. It doesn't matter where, but clear your head and put your shoulders down.... and off you go.

Kirsty Wark, Journalist/Author

Performance anxiety coping tips (although they can often be used to deal with every day anxiety I have found). Acknowledge it. Don't try and pretend that the anxiety is not happening. The more you deny anxiety, the stronger it gets. Simply try and take note that it is happening and at all costs, keep going. If you concede defeat, you will set a mental precedent, which will make it all the harder the next time.

Move
Try moving physically to a different spot, or at least change the focus of your vision. I find sometimes a simple look away or down can mentally 'reset' my brain and deal with the surge of adrenalin that comes with the 'fight or flight' response. Be as natural as you can be and as fluid in your movements as possible, as this can help to reassure your mind that everything is in fact ok.

Appendices - Shared Experience

Keep Calm
You *can* stay in control, because you *are* in control. You do not have a disease of the nervous system which can overtake your will, as with Sydenham's chorea or Tourettes Syndrome, it is a matter of a primal response to fear, the desire to panic and run away from a perceived threat. *You* are in control of your brain, not the other way around, realize that and if anxiety hits, accept it and determine to do the next right thing anyway. Your brain will soon get the message.

Avoid booze the night before
Hangovers put a lot of pressure on the nervous system, as do drugs, caffeine and lack of sleep. My anxiety is ALWAYS worse when I'm tired. Give your body a helping hand by abstaining before a big event, and make sure you get plenty of rest and plenty of water.

Watch your pace
When people get anxious, they often unconsciously speed up the pace of their speech or actions to try and get the event over with. However this sends a clear message to the brain that something is wrong and it will act accordingly. Just keep your pace steady and deliberate and the experience will be much more enjoyable.

Eat
My anxiety is always very much at the fore when I'm hungry. For me there is a real connection between my anxiety and my blood sugar. I think the shaky feeling of hunger makes my body think it's anxious. Have a banana, not a fry up, just enough to keep you topped up until the end.

Trust yourself
Chances are you've done this before and survived, what would possibly change that this time? Your brain will play tricks on you and tell you THIS is the time it will all fall apart, it's not true, you're the same person as last time and if you got through it then, you can again.

If it's your first time, still trust, you may have dealt with much worse in the past, deaths, births, financial troubles or illness. You got through. You got this. In either event TRUST YOURSELF.

John Jack, Actor/Coach

Appendices - Shared Experience

(2) PERSONAL TIPS FROM LAWYERS

1. *Note to self – preparing for proof*
   Amber Galbraith, Advocate, Compass Chambers, Faculty of Advocates.

2. *The art of persuasion*
   Kate Dowdalls Q.C., Arnott Manderson Stable, Faculty of Advocates.

3. *Dealing with a difficult judge*
   Robert Milligan Q.C., Compass Chambers, Faculty of Advocates.

4. *Examination and cross-examination of experts*
   Geoff Clarke Q.C., Compass Chambers, Faculty of Advocates.

5. *Cross-examination*
   Peter Crooks, Solicitor/Advocate, Bonnar Accident Law.

6. *Discrediting a witness by using prior statements*
   Dorothy Bain Q.C., Ampersand Stable, Faculty of Advocates.

Appendices - Shared Experience

1. Note to self ….. preparing for proof

Work backwards

Preparing for a proof can be daunting. You may have screeds of papers, and there will be lots of thoughts, ideas and lines floating around your head – you will be desperate to get cracking on working out your killer questions for the key witnesses. But, as with any journey, before you start you should make sure you know where you are going.

To make sure that your preparation is as effective as it can be, it is advisable to keep focussed on what you are going to be asking the Court to do at the end of the proof and why - ie what the issues are, what evidence supports your case, and why you are asking the Court to accept it. You need to know from the start what evidence you will need to bring out and what evidence you want to bury, obscure or minimise. There are often many tangents and red herrings during a proof, and if you have a careful plan of what is important, and what is irrelevant, drafted from the outset it should help you to focus and out-manoeuvre your opponent.

For that reason, I find it is usually helpful to have a 'master' document, setting out the analysis of the case. If you list out the key points/issues of dispute (if you can, use the same terminology as is used in the pleadings), then under each heading you can proceed to list the good and bad pieces of evidence relating to each (documents, witness or both), and think about how you are going to bring it out most effectively. This document is something you can keep with you throughout the case, and check off as you go to make sure you have everything you need as you go along.

Once you have that case analysis, it will normally provide a good basis for drafting outline submissions. When preparing for proof, I'd strongly recommend drafting submissions first, before working back and preparing lines of questioning for the witnesses. That way, you know what you need to ask each witness and why. Once you have an outline for all these documents, you'll probably dip in and out of each, making changes as you go through your prep.

Write it down

Don't wing it. We've all seen brilliant lawyers standing up without an apparent note, and enthralling judge or jury with fabulously articulate and persuasive arguments. But, I'd like to bet most (if not all) will have prepared and thought very carefully about exactly what they want to say, when and how – and have most probably written it all down at some stage. Many sheriffs of judges will now require written submissions in any event. However, just going through that process of ordering your thoughts and words will help your final delivery – even if you don't ultimately want, or need, to rely on notes.

This applies to aspects of the proof, from examination-in-chief, cross-examination to submissions. Indeed, one of the best pieces of advice I ever got was to write down all the questions I wanted to ask in cross-examination beforehand – although we all like to think that killer 'Perry Mason' question will come to us spontaneously during a witness's evidence, the reality is that is very unlikely and a question thought about and formulated carefully in the quiet of your office will be much more effective than one that occurs in the heat of battle. It is all too easy to get carried away with excitement and enthusiasm on the day, and to end up bringing out un-helpful or damaging evidence. Having a written list means you have a good structure to the evidence, can end on your strongest point, keep control of the witness and you can cross off questions if the relevant piece of evidence is brought out earlier. Remember, don't ask any more questions than you absolutely have to! Many a good Court-lawyer has become unstuck by asking just one question too many. Less is more.

Know the case/papers

Sounds obvious, I know, but it is vital to have a thorough knowledge not only of the legal and factual issues in the case, but also to know in detail all the productions that have been lodged (for both sides) and make sure all copies have been numbered the same way. You should keep an inventory of process handy, so you know what has been lodged and when.

When you are going through the productions during your preparation, a chronology is often very helpful, with cross-references to documents where the evidence can be found.

Some of us are tidier than others, but from experience it is so much easier when preparing if you try and keep your papers in an order that you are familiar with and can easily navigate your way around. You will get to know how you like your papers organised, and it's just a matter of finding out what works best for you.

I have found stationery to be a sound investment when preparing for proof – in particular, having a fine array of coloured sticky notes is invaluable, perhaps using a particular colour for different issues in the case. That said, don't be too enthusiastic and end up with a fluttering mass of jubilee bunting, where you can't actually find anything.

Part of knowing the case is often also knowing your opponent. If you can, try and make contact well in advance of the proof, to establish their approach and to see if matters can be focussed or agreed.

Preparation is the key to a well-conducted proof – sadly, there are no short-cuts. The better prepared you are, the more confident you tend to feel on the day (even with a ropey case) – and, be warned, there is rarely a more horrific feeling than going into a proof feeling under-prepared… Good luck!

Amber Galbraith
Advocate

Appendices - Shared Experience

2. The art of persuasion

If I had been asked to explain the purpose of oral advocacy when I was a law student in the early 80's, I would have been at a loss to explain. I might have muttered something about asking questions and representing clients' interests. I might even have said that it was all about telling the court what your case is. What I would not have said is that the purpose of oral advocacy is the creation of an event of your choosing in the mind of the decision maker. Asking questions and telling the court about your case are essential elements in what I now understand is "the art of persuasion", but there is so much more to the practice of the art of oral advocacy than those basic elements.

Many years of training and experience later, I understand far better the importance of oral advocacy. I have the tools and skills that enable me to be an effective advocate. I can assess what works and what doesn't. I can get through a submission or examination of a witness with apparent competence. It's not magic, and it's not a talent I was born with. It takes hard work, preparation, planning and practice.

You are, presumably, reading this book because you want to be a better advocate. You want to present your case to the sheriff efficiently and with skill. You want to persuade the sheriff to make the decision most favourable to your client. Here are some hints and tips that I hope will help you to achieve your goal.

There is no case that cannot be improved by the use of good stationery! Yes, seriously. Post-its and highlighters, folders and dividers will make the presentation of your case easier. Use them to organize and marshall your papers. Mark up significant passages of evidence or in legislation and authorities so that you can find them quickly. Cross-reference the productions for a trial or proof. Arrange the papers in a way that allows you to identify what you need and refer to it with apparent ease and efficiency.

Know and understand the case and the materials that you will be relying on. Read the Record. Familiarise yourself with the productions – yours and your opponent's. Read the statements and precognitions of witnesses. Read and understand any experts' reports – if you don't understand, ask your expert.

Make a plan

You may not want or need to stick rigidly to the plan, but knowing it is there will give you confidence. There is no need to write down every word you intend to say or every question you want to ask, but it might help. At least, note the points that you intend to cover in in your submissions or during examination of witnesses.

Be aware

Pay attention to the sheriff. Is he / she writing down what you / the witness are saying? Are you making eye contact? Is he / she watching and listening to the witness?
Does the witness understand your questions? Listen to the answers.

Take your time

Can the sheriff note your submissions / the evidence? If not, slow down or pause to allow him / her to catch up.

Keep it simple

Stick to one fact per question. Use short sentences. Think about the language that you are using. Be precise.

Don't ask a question unless you know the answer.

Be prepared!

I could, of course, go on. These are basic strategies for successful advocacy. Once you are in the habit of using these, your skills will develop, as will your confidence. It is a privilege to be allowed to address the court and represent the interests of clients. The better prepared you are, the more effective your advocacy will be. Good luck – and enjoy!

Kate Dowdalls QC

Appendices - Shared Experience

3. Dealing with a difficult judge

Being in court is difficult and stressful at the best of times. A considerate judge who knows what they are doing and wants to achieve the right result with the minimum of fuss can go a long way to minimising that stress. Conversely, a difficult judge can make a tough job next to impossible.

Fortunately, most modern judges fall into the former category. However, particularly when you are new to court, at some point you will come across a judge who seems to be going out of their way to make your life miserable. How do you cope with that?

The first thing to work out is why they are behaving in the way they are. There are generally 3 possible causes. The first is you. The second is your argument. The third is the judge.

The first possible reason is that your argument is tenuous or unappealing to the judge. If that is the case there is little you can do. It is part of a court lawyer's job to present their client's case, however, unsympathetic it may be, unless it is unstateable. Sometimes this will mean making a submission in which you have little confidence. There are certain phrases that make it clear that you are simply doing your job e.g. "I am instructed to argue that...". Equally, it is a good idea at the outset of a difficult argument to make it clear to the judge that you recognise the size of your challenge. At least that way the judge knows that you are aware of the problems with your case and that reminding you of them every 2 minutes is not going to help anyone.

The second possible reason is that the way you are presenting your argument is irritating the judge. Most of us have certain foibles or idiosyncrasies, particularly under pressure, that can be annoying to others. In training the Devils, the Faculty of Advocates provides video analysis which can be a chastening experience. Be aware of this possibility and if you see the judge looking at you angrily as you fiddle with your pen, put it down!

The final possibility, and the one that presents the greatest challenge, is that the judge is in a bad temper. This may be a temporary state of affairs or a permanent one. In the latter case it is usually possible to find out in advance if you are facing the prospect of a long day in court. Such judges, because they are few and far between, are generally fairly notorious. You just have to console yourself with the knowledge that most bullies are insecure and the real reason they are giving you a hard time is because of their own inadequacies.

More difficult is the unexpectedly grumpy judge. As always, a bit of preparation goes a long way. There is never any harm in speaking to the clerk beforehand to find out what the judge thinks of the case or whether they have identified any particular difficulties in advance. If there is something else on in court before you, you will quickly see if the judge is out for blood.

Whatever the reason is for the judge being difficult, it is essential to remain calm and polite. Rudeness should never be met with rudeness. When I first started at the Bar I heard a no doubt apocryphal story of a solicitor who, when asked by the sheriff whether he was trying to show his contempt for the court, answered "No, I am trying to hide it." Responses like this should under no circumstances be spoken out loud! Everyone has bad days in court and in many ways it is how you handle adversity that really marks you out as a proper litigator.

Robert Milligan Q.C.

4. Examination and cross-examination of experts

In examination-in-chief don't forget to have your expert identify and adopt all that is said in his or her report. If you have a good expert it's tempting just to leave presentation to him or her. That's okay but use questions such as "one of your main propositions was x, just how important is x?" Or "You have given us quite a lot of information there, can I attempt to break it down..."

In cross remember that experts will know more than you. So try and pin them down to those facts they have relied upon and only after that suggest other facts they should have taken into account. If you can offer an escape route, do, for instance; "Mr X this is an area where there is some overlap between vascular surgery and orthopaedics, if I ask a question which you think would be better directed to an orthopaedic surgeon, please just say so."

You need to ask your own expert in advance what is important, what alternative views may be expressed and what documents can be produced to gainsay them. The internet is a great resource and should be looked at but, ideally, not solely relied upon.

Experts are professionals who, generally, are trying to assist the Court. You will get no points for trying to embarrass them. Don't be afraid to say "Well can I ask you to explain that?" Then listen and logically test the answer. Hopefully that will allow your own expert to treat whatever is said as a rare exception or enable the opinion to be explained away and mean your side will prevail.

Geoff Clarke Q.C.

5. Cross-examination

There are two purposes to cross-examination. The first is to establish and advance your own case. The second is to challenge the opponent's case involving either discrediting the evidence or discrediting the witness. When cross-examining a witness you need to bear in mind that most of them are not lying. They are often trying to provide an account of the events as they saw them. You should therefore be careful if you decide to attack them as untruthful. Here are a few points:-

The cross-examination needs to be structured through appropriate planning. My preparation usually involves particular subject areas which the witnesses can be crossed on. Keep the cross to points which support your theory of the case. This will strengthen your argument.

Before you cross-examine a witness you need to consider whether the evidence they have provided in chief is harmful to your case. There is little point in trying to undermine a witness who has provided favourable evidence. If a witness during chief has said something which favours your case, then during cross you should make the witness repeat it for emphasis.

Make your strongest points at the beginning and end of your cross-examination.

Always listen carefully to the witness's answer and observe the witness' demeanour when giving their evidence in cross.

Note taking: your focus should be on observing the witness's demeanour during questioning, listening to and focussing upon the answers given and re-structuring or adding to) the points that you have prepared for the cross-examination or in light of the answers given by the witness. Ideally, you should have a colleague such as a trainee or para-legal who is there to assist you in court by taking verbatim notes if possible of each witnesses' evidence. There may, however, be crucial answers given to questions which you wish to note down. Although a shorthand writer is present during ordinary cause proofs in the sheriff court and evidence is recorded in the court of session, it is not the norm for the notes to be transcribed. Answers given by witnesses are critically important when you are preparing submissions, particularly if you are preparing written submissions.

Appendices - Shared Experience

I have watched various proofs in the sheriff court and court of session over the years. In my view, almost without exception, the most effective cross-examiners are those who are not aggressive, but firm and courteous to the witness.

If the witness refuses to directly answer a question, simply keep on repeating the question. If there comes a point where the judge reacts unfavourably to you, you simply have to make the point that the witness is refusing to properly answer the question.

Only leading questions should be asked. The only occasions you should ask an open question are where the point is uncontroversial, or (and you need to be very careful about this) you know that the only possible answer the witness can give is not going to be prejudicial to your case. You should be seeking to control the witness's evidence during cross at all times.

If a witness's evidence has been harmful to your case in chief, then in cross-examining them you should seek to either challenge their evidence as inconsistent, improbably or unrealistic, or you should challenge the witness as mistaken or untruthful. This is where previous documentary evidence relating to the witness, which contradicts their evidence in chief, can be put to them. For example you should look for any inconsistency of what a witness has said during proof and what they have said in a prior statement. If there are any differences, you should ask the witness to repeat the fact which they gave in their evidence in chief and then read out the part of the previous statement which is inconsistent and ask the witness if they made that statement. On the other hand if there is no previous inconsistent statement or other piece of documentary evidence, it is best to focus upon the manner in which they saw the event. For example, from a distance, poor weather conditions, only got a quick glimpse of the event etc.

Should you ask the 'ultimate' question: should you put your version of the case to the witness and give them the chance to accept or deny? In America, trial lawyers are taught not to do that. In Scotland, under the rule that your case should be put to your opponent, my own view is that the ultimate question should be asked with the witness required to either accept or deny it.

Peter Crooks
Solicitor Advocate

Appendices - Shared Experience

6. Discrediting a witness by using prior statements

To be an effective trial lawyer you require to master the technique of discrediting a witness by reference to a previous statement they have made. You must be able to do this with ease, confidence and precision. The only way to achieve this is to work at perfecting what is a relatively straightforward technique – and getting lots and lots of practice.

Practice is often available to those regularly conducting criminal trial work. For civil practitioners not so fortunate to get into court on a regular basis, lack of court room experience can be overcome by detailed preparation and understanding the correct technique.

So, how do you discredit by reference to prior statements? I suggest by following the technique known as; *"Commit, Credit and Confront"*.

What do I mean by commit? This is to commit the witness to the evidence they have given in court.

Why do you do this? It is to close off any avenue the witness may seek to find to avoid answering the important point; also known as "closing the gates". It is essential to pin the witness down and have it made clear to the court what he or she has said in evidence. This is required in order that the contrast with the prior statement, when it is made, is obvious to the fact finder.

How do you do commit? You take great care in listening to the witness's evidence and in noting what they have said accurately. Thereafter, when it comes to the examination of the witness, you must also be accurate at recounting the evidence they have given, as not only the witness but probably your opponent, and perhaps the Judge, will correct you. It really can water down the effect of your examination if you are constantly interrupted or corrected on what the witness previously said. You are no longer in control, you are obviously not on top of things and the witness has the upper hand before you have embarked on the most important part of what you are doing. So do take care in noting the evidence and recounting it accurately.

The next stage is to credit the prior statement, by perhaps;

Appendices - Shared Experience

(a) the circumstances in which it was taken,
(b) the timing of the prior statement, and
(c) the purpose or reason that the prior statement was given in the first place.

So why commit and, why credit? It is to demonstrate to the fact finder that the previous statement you are relying contains the truth and therefore the version in court is not to be accepted. Ultimately, in this exercise, you must not just discredit for the sake of it or indeed just to show your brilliant technique. You must take care, plan ahead and be working towards your final submission. Do not just attack the witness for the sake of it – a simple example; you said in your statement the accused was wearing brown shoes when in fact today you said he was wearing black shoes – that is pointless and takes away the force of what you are trying to achieve. Further, do not challenge the witness if the difference between what they said in evidence and what the stated previously will make no difference to your final submission. You can, in that situation, come across as argumentative and you may lose sympathy for your position.

How do you credit the prior statement? The process of crediting is one of picture painting and it shows that the circumstances in which the previous statement were given demonstrate that it is more likely to contain the truth.

You require to take care as to form and content of your questions; use closed questions, precise language, one fact per question and facts not conclusions. These simple rules of advocacy apply to this process just as much as they do to others.

And in the process of crediting you can use either or both "external" and "internal" crediting. By external, I am referring to the circumstances in which the statement was made; the day after the event or at the time of the event, when you were at home, when you were sober and when you read it over and signed it on each page. By reference to internal, I am making reference to external facts that support the statement; for example in the statement the witness speaks to seeing an event immediately before the crucial event your case is concerned with. Demonstrating the truth and accuracy of what the witness has spoken to immediately prior to the crucial event will give greater credit to the information he or she passed on about the crucial event; proved by physical recoveries from a locus or the contents of a text message or the recordings made by CCTV.

Internal crediting may require you to prove in evidence certain facts before you lead the witness and this therefore means you have to take care about the stage you call the witness. In order to make your examination all the more powerful you may wish the fact finder to know about the other evidence first.

So you have committed the witness and you have credited the statement - the next stage is to confront the witness. In order to do this you have to know the content of your prior statement extremely well – this can take many hours of preparation. As much as is possible, you will have worked out in advance the passages that you will wish to put to the witness. Do not read out huge sections of the statement. To make your point, and get it across effectively, go to the part you are making reference to as quickly as possible but always ensuring that it will make sense.

During the conduct of your examination, read the portion of the statement you are seeking to challenge the witness over out yourself. I do not recommend that the witness be asked to read it out. This way, you remain in control of the examination and you can put your own emphasis on what is recorded – hand this part of the exercise over to a hostile witness and it creates problems and allows them to take control.

You then confront the witness by pointing out that the statement is different. How force fully you do that, what emphasis you seek to make may depend upon the witness - and you will reasonably conclude I am sure that how you approach the respectable accountant who is mistaken about what he has seen or remembers and, the dishonest fraudster or the accused's friends who are lying to cover up for him will require a difference in approach.

Another method that is frequently used is it to point out that the witness is now saying something that is not in his statement. I have seen practitioners telling the witness to read the statement and confirm nothing of what he has just said is recorded in his previous statement. I think whilst this is plainly something that can be done, it is not really a safe way of proceeding and not nearly as effective as reading out the relevant part or the part at which it was reasonable to expect the witness to say precisely what he is saying now and then following it up by emphasising the fact that he or she did not say this before.

Appendices - Shared Experience

The final stage - the "WHY" question. Having followed the technique I suggest, and having pointed out the difference between the prior statement and the witness's evidence, do you follow up with the witness the reason why the evidence is different, or do you leave that for final submission? It very much depends on your approach and the tactic you wish to adopt; it also depends upon your experience and the degree to which you consider you can control the witness. Whatever you decide, be cautious and confident that you can manage the outcome, as poor technique and losing control of the situation at this final stage of your examination may undo all the good work.

Finally, knowledge of the law requires to be combined with the technique I have described. In civil procedure the whole thing is relatively easy as there is no rule against the eliciting of hearsay evidence. However in criminal law it is different. It is a complex area of law that you should take time to find out about before you begin to embark on this process in the criminal trial court.

Dorothy Bain Q.C.

Bibliography

Arredondo, L. (1991) *How to Present like a Pro.* McGraw-Hill, Inc.

Atkinson, Professor M. *Lend me your ears.* Vermillion.

Berkley, S. (2004) *Speak to Influence.* Campbell Hall Press.

Berry, C. (2003) *Voice and the Actor.* Virgin Books Ltd.

Carey, D & RC Carey RC. (2008) *Vocal Arts Workbook and dvd.* Methuen/drama.

Dalby, J. (1993) *How to Speak well in Business.* Aardvark Press.

Davies, P. (1991) *Your Total Image.* Piatkus (Publishers) Ltd.

Houseman, B. (2002) *Finding Your Voice.* Nick Hern Books.

Houseman, B. (2011) *Tackling Text.* Nick Hern Books.

Lubar, K & Halpern BL. (2003) *Leadership Presence.* Gotham Books.

Rodenburg, P. (2009) *Power Presentation.* Penguin/Michael Joseph.

Rodenburg, P. (1998) *The Actor Speaks.* Methuen.

Roland, Dr. D. (2001) *The Confident Performer.* Nick Hern Books.

Stuart, C. (2000) *Speak for Yourself.* Piatkus (Publishers) Ltd.

Turk, C. (1991) *Effective Speaking.* E&FN Spon.

Janine Willis and Alexander Todorov, (2006) Psychological Science research article, *First Impressions: Making Up Your Mind After a 100-Ms Exposure to a Face,* Princeton University.

Selected Legal Bibliography

Keith Evans, (2004) *Common Sense Rules of Advocacy for Lawyers*

Charles Hennessy, (2006) *Practical Advocacy in the Sheriff Court*

Michael Hyam, (1999) *Advocacy Skills*

Brian Johnson and Marsha Hunter, (2009) *The Articulate Advocate*

Steven Lubet, (2000) *Modern Trial Advocacy*

Robin McEwan, (1995) *Pleading in Court*

John Munkman, (1991) *The Technique of Advocacy*

D Shane Read, (2007) *Winning at Trial*

David Ross, (2007) *Advocacy*

Herbert J. Stern, (1991-1999) *Trying Cases to Win,* 5 volumes